Ruth & Skitch Henderson's Christmas in the Country

Recipes, Crafts, Gifts, and Music

Ruth & Skitch Henderson
and Judith Blahnik

Photographs by
Lans Christensen

Design by Joseph Rutt

VIKING STUDIO BOOKS

VIKING STUDIO BOOKS
Published by the Penguin Group
Penguin Books USA Inc., 375 Hudson Street,
New York, New York 10014, U.S.A.
Penguin Books Ltd, 27 Wrights Lane,
London W8 5TZ, England
Penguin Books Australia Ltd, Ringwood,
Victoria, Australia
Penguin Books Canada Ltd, 10 Alcorn Avenue,
Toronto, Ontario, Canada M4V 3B2
Penguin Books (N.Z.) Ltd, 182–190 Wairau Road,
Auckland 10, New Zealand

Penguin Books Ltd, Registered Offices:
Harmondsworth, Middlesex, England

First published in 1993 by Viking Penguin,
a division of Penguin Books USA Inc.

1 3 5 7 9 10 8 6 4 2

Photograph credits
Pages 4 (below), 10 (below), 80 (top right and below right), 84, 86 (left and right), 87
(left), 107, 144, 168 (top right and middle right): Ruth and Skitch Henderson; pages 11
(top right and below right), 80 (below left), 87 (top right), and 143: Stephen
Green–Armytage; pages 80 (top left), 82 (top left and right): © Steve J. Sherman; page
83 (below): Tim Lee; page 125 (top): NBC.

ISBN 0-670-84783-6

CIP data is available

Printed in Hong Kong
Set in Perpetua
Designed by Joseph Rutt

For our children, Hans and Heidi, and their families
For Peter Dubos and Sandy Daniels and Susan York and our Silo family
For Peter Lane and Karen, Mark, and Wai and our New York Pops family
For Eileen FitzGerald, Cathy French, and June Freemanzon—our extended family
And in memory of Dimitri, our Siberian husky, who lived
to be seventeen and a half years old in total freedom

ACKNOWLEDGMENTS

Nineteen ninety-three was a milestone year. Skitch celebrated his seventy-fifth birthday, Ruth and Skitch celebrated their thirty-fifth year of marriage, the New York Pops Orchestra marked a healthy tenth anniversary, and the Silo came of age with twenty-one years of service to our customers, twenty-one years of cooking and baking, and twenty-one years of arts and crafts in the Gallery.

We would like to thank all who have helped us and have been so willing to share our memories and our daily lives, especially Fay Fitch, who so splendidly cares for us and our animal family, and Bud Bostwick, our neighbor who grew up on this farm and now gives tons of advice to us and refuge to one or the other of our dogs.

Thank you, Peter Dubos, for your creativity, which you so generously give.

Thank you, Sandy Daniels, for your energy and organization and the forever delicious and endless variety of cookies.

Thank you, Barrie Kavasch, for introducing us to our Native American friends, who have inspired us with their traditions and spirit.

Thank you, Richard Hill, for cutting all those trees and flowers to dry, for harvesting the pine cones, and for the hundreds of Christmas lights everywhere.

Thank you, Susan York, for the thousands of things you've done for us for the past ten years—Happy Anniversary!

Thank you, Michael Fragnito, for walking into the Silo Gallery at Christmas and asking us on the spot to do this book.

Thank you, Joseph Rutt, for coming into our lives and understanding us instantly.

Finally, to the "Dream Team"—Barbara Williams, our editor, Judith Blahnik, our co-writer and co-conspirator, and Lans Christensen, our photographer, friend, and neighbor—working with all of you is a joy.

Contents

❧ ❧

By Way of Introduction

We live on a farm. Actually, we live on two farms, which were built very close together during the early 1800s in New Milford, Connecticut, in the Litchfield Hills. We call it Hunt Hill Farm.

We bought the two farms nearly twenty-five years ago—the first one was originally owned by the Anderson family, who were dairy farmers descended from early Swedish settlers. The second was owned by Bud Bostwick, a farmer descended from John Bostwick, who settled here in 1707. Bud is still our closest neighbor and on any afternoon he and Skitch can be seen walking the land together, Skitch listening intently to Bud's stories of early New Milford.

We have come to love the town and the history here. In 1702, fourteen Indians signed a land deed in exchange for "sixty pounds current money in the colony of Connecticut and twenty pounds of goods." Since then, the Plantation of New Milford, as it was called until 1773, has grown into the largest "landtown common" in Connecticut, measuring 64.4 square miles. It has attracted settlers from all over the world, including one of our most historically important citizens, Roger Sherman, who moved here in 1743 from Newton, Massachusetts. Sherman's purported original house is now the Roger Sherman Town Hall in New Milford.

Our Hunt Hill Farm is located in what was once called the North Purchase—New Milford's land expansion, acquired in 1722. Today, Northville is its name. There are two large farmhouses and a tenant farmer's cottage here, all about 160 years old. We call one the 1836

◆1◆

ABOVE: *Weathered wood fences are a signature of Hunt Hill Farm. Dreading the day when we might have to replace them with new ones, Ruth buys discarded railing and fence posts from old farms whenever she can—just to keep a stockpile for repairs and replacements.*

FAR LEFT: *The Silo Store, Gallery, and Cooking School has its entrance next to this silo, one of four at Hunt Hill Farm. We left some silage still visible on the natural wood inside.*

House, named for the year that it was built. Rambling and roomy, it was big enough for the Bostwicks and has ample space today for our daughter, Heidi, when she comes to visit with her young sons, Sam and Will.

The other farmhouse, which we call the Main House, is the original Anderson family home, where our son, Hans, our daughter-in-law, Sandra, and our grandchildren Keiran and Kythera live. In Hunt Hill Cottage, originally built for a tenant farmer, our friend June Freemanzon spends her weekends.

We make our home in what was once the Bostwick cow barn, feed loft, and grain silos. We call it the 1836 Barn. The L-shaped red

exterior looks very much as it did when Ralph Buckingham, a relative of the Bostwicks, built it in the early 1800s. We have renovated the interior, creating a living room, which we call the Great Room, that has a sleeping loft for guests. We have three bedrooms, four bathrooms, two office spaces, and a large open kitchen with extended dining and living areas. There's a cozy round breakfast room on one floor of the old grain silo and a relaxing hot tub on the ground floor of the same silo.

Mr. Buckingham's hand-hewn chestnut timber is visible everywhere, as we tried to leave as much as we could of the original barn frame, walls, and flooring. Its honest, rustic character makes a warm home for us and an authentic space to house our collections of antique toys, pottery, farm tables, chests, and wood carvings.

Other original buildings include machinery sheds, stables, a tobacco barn, a cook shed (our addition, to accommodate Skitch's passion for outdoor cooking), and a poolhouse next to the swimming pool. We have a pond where wild ducks nest in spring, bass thrive in summer, and the children ice-skate in winter. Everything

ABOVE: *Isabelle, outside the 1836 Barn, watches the corner of Upland Road, where Skitch makes the turn for home.* LEFT: *This painting of our farm by Janice Harding Owens was a Christmas surprise for Ruth cooked up by Skitch and his Kentucky banker friend John Irvin, who finds and nourishes Kentucky artists and craftspersons. In the upper left is Skitch's tractor barn; to the right is the pond. The old carriage house below and to the left is now the pool house, and below it on the right is the Main House. To its immediate left is Hunt Hill Cottage. The set of barns and the barnyard below and to the left is now the Silo Store, Gallery, and Cooking School. Across from it is the 1836 House; below are our horse pasture, riding ring, and stable. To their left is the 1836 Barn.*

❖ 3 ❖

and everyone is connected by short, well-worn paths and a gravel road.

In the summertime, we harvest the several gardens, which give us baskets of vegetables, a vast array of perennial flowers, and bunches of herbs and berries. In wintertime, we ward off the darkness with extra candles, some burning in glasses, some behind stained glass, some in chandeliers. Outside, we string tiny white lights across railings or over the branches of a small evergreen standing alone in the cold.

The other large barn, the original Anderson barn, is the reason many people take the turn off Route 202 onto Upland Road to come see us. The Silo Store, Cooking School, and Gallery are housed in what once was the cow barn, loft, and stables. The Silo has become a must-see place in northwestern Connecticut if one has the same appetite for good food, art, and celebrating that we do. The store stocks and sells unusual as well as basic cookware and tableware, and the large, airy gallery features the work of artisans, craftspeople, painters, and sculptors from all over the country. Chefs and cookbook authors teach in the Silo Cooking School, filling up classes almost year-round—spring, summer, fall, and early winter. In 1992, we all proudly celebrated the Silo's twentieth birthday!

ABOVE LEFT: *An eight-man wooden scull from Hans's crewing days at Rumsey Hall School hangs above the tobacco barn doors. Inside the barn, we dry hydrangeas and wild flowers and spread out piles of pine cones, gourds, and acorns on old screens. Skitch's barbecue shed is in the distance.*

LEFT: *From our family album, here is a photo by our friend Georgia Sheron. We are standing in the horse pasture with the 1836 Barn and silos in the background. Our dog Sheba loves the snow. Alma, our King Charles Spaniel, always preferred summers.*

ABOVE RIGHT: *This weather vane has a commanding view of the Silo barnyard and Heidi's pony stable, which is now filled with Silo crafts and pottery.*

RIGHT: *The windows of the Silo Store display tins for stollen, daisy-shaped cake molds, ice cream molds, tart rings, bread pans, ladyfinger tins, and Kugelhopf pans. Once a cow stable, the store now houses a huge selection of cookware and bakeware.*

Christmas at Hunt Hill Farm

❧ ❧

Christmas for us starts early—really early! The February before, Ruth must begin ordering Christmas merchandise for the Silo Store. Skitch must put his mind on Christmas as early as June, when his final plans for programming the New York Pops holiday concerts at Carnegie Hall are due.

In a way, Christmas is in our heads a good part of the year. Early in October, we set up the big Christmas tree, cut from the farm, in the Silo Gallery for the Gallery of Gifts. From that moment on, all hearts beat a little faster. By November, the Silo Gallery has become a wonderland of gifts, ornaments, wreaths, chocolate Santas, Advent calendars, and tins of holiday sweets and savories. People come from all over to see the tree and to buy the one-of-a-kind ornaments, handcrafted gifts, American and imported holiday foods, and local gourmet goodies.

By the time Thanksgiving comes, we begin our own family preparations for Christmas. Ruth will put up any leftover cranberry sauce, thinking ahead of someone who might like a gift from the kitchen. We all take walks to collect the final harvest of fall—baskets of pine cones in all shapes and sizes, some still sticky with pitch, some thick and long and open with strong spines and woody petals, some small and round. We haul in bare tree branches, moss, wild grasses and flowers, thistles, and tree mushrooms. All of it will dry in time to have another life, either tied to a package as part of a wrapping or shaped into wreaths, arranged in vases and hung with a few ornaments, or piled in bowls and baskets just to look pretty and give cheer.

❖7❖

ABOVE: *Heirloom stockings, designed by Judie Tasch, make memorable gifts. This is the one we gave to our gallery director, Peter Dubos, with instructions to bring it back each year for a refill.*

FAR LEFT: *After a big winter storm, the trees take on a new stillness—so laden with snow the branches don't move at all. We love the quiet that then sets in over the farm.*

We mark and celebrate the Sundays of Advent—those four Sundays before Christmas—just as Ruth did as a child in Germany. In the Advent tradition, there is one special wreath among all the wreaths that adorn the farm—the Advent wreath for the Sunday ritual at the main meal. Each Sunday, a new candle is added to the wreath and lit, bringing more and more light into the darkest time of the year.

The time of Advent reverberates with memories for Ruth and is the basis for many of our family traditions. During her childhood, it was an exciting time of waiting and preparing—when appetites grew along with great anticipation. There was a flurry of activity during the day, and at night the evenings were cozy, perfumed by fresh evergreens that Ruth's mother placed in tall vases, shaped into

wreaths, or strung into garlands. As the weeks progressed, decorations would gradually come down from the attic. First, the little hand-carved *Räuchermänner* (men smoking pipes), who burned incense on small tin plates in their bellies while smoke curled from their mouths. There were a hunter, a carpenter, and a mushroom picker. Then the nutcrackers appeared—soldiers and a Santa—with crocks of nuts. The house came alive with a new look and feel, and always with the smell of fresh evergreens.

For Skitch, ever since he turned sixteen, Christmastime has been spent on the road. First as a piano player, then later, with his own band, he worked through the holiday time, traveling from one club date to another. It wasn't a particularly comforting experience. After providing musical cheer for audiences, the band would return to the hotel in whatever small town they were in to no particular festivities. Home cooking was certainly a rarity. Once, while Skitch was on holiday tour with the young Frank Sinatra, Frank's mother brought dinner—homemade manicotti for the whole band. It was a rare feast and a great Christmas present.

ABOVE LEFT: *Hand-carved replicas of the* Raüchermänner, *sometimes called "incense men," that Ruth remembers from her childhood are now available in this country.*

ABOVE: *Two nutcrackers stand ready for duty. A crock or bowl full of nuts is a welcoming sight for visitors and makes a good gift with or without a nutcracker.*

TOP: *When a local church was renovated and made into a theater, Skitch and our good friend Eileen FitzGerald rescued the organ, transporting it to the farm in a horse trailer. Here it resides, reassembled in the loft above the Great Room in the 1836 Barn.* ABOVE: *Daly's Dandelion was a landmark watering hole on East 61st Street in New York City and was our first restaurant and bar. At Christmastime it was often a place of solace for neighborhood regulars.*

Bringing music into people's lives became a round-the-clock occupation during the holidays. But soon after we married, Christmastime became a more personal season. There was still the grueling concert schedule, but there were always bits of time to steal and spend at home—even if it was only an afternoon to take the kids skating. After we opened Daly's Dandelion, our first restaurant in New York, Skitch would make it a point to be there as often as he could during the season, dropping in unexpectedly, extending his own personal hospitality. A good wholesome meal in a friendly and spirited atmosphere meant a lot to people in the thick of the Christmas rush, and it was always heartening to chat with the Daly's regulars. For some of them, it was their only home for the holidays. In the old neighborhood, Skitch would lead our 61st and 62nd Street neighbors in a carol sing from door to door. When we moved to New Milford, he helped organize the first-ever town carol sing on the green, which Mr. Bayer, conductor of the New Milford High School Band, has taken over and which has become an annual tradition.

The weeks in between our Advent Sundays are as busy as anyone else's—filled with cooking, baking, handicrafts, wreath-making, planting the hyacinth, paperwhite, and amaryllis bulbs that will blossom indoors in their pots, for gifts, and packaging presents to send all over the world, always with a pine cone from the farm included. The 1836 Barn comes to life with carols or Skitch's favorite Christmas music. We take time to skate on the pond with the grandchildren and, afterward, to come in together to the smells of the kitchen—vanilla, cinnamon, toasted almonds, and sweet citrus.

The kitchens of the Main House, the 1836 Barn, and Hunt Hill cottage are busy, fragrant places during Advent. We all share in the work, preparations, and meals. Sometimes there's a snack for us all at Junie's cottage. Always, it seems, there's an inviting fire at Hans and Sandra's, and usually a one-pot meal in the making at the 1836 Barn.

Much of what we do together to celebrate the season here on the farm comes from our great appreciation for family, friends, good food, art, and music. And much of what we do is also based in curiosity, a kind of openness to trying something new.

We wrote this book to bring to life our memories of holidays past and to share how we live nowadays during a busy, joyous season. We have ideas for entertaining, decorations, simple gifts for friends, hearty winter meals for family, and projects that bring people together. Perhaps our stories of Christmas in the country will jog your memory, fire your imagination, and enrich your Christmas wherever you live.

LEFT: *Small gingerbread houses with individual names scrolled on rooftops make great gifts or place markers at a holiday dinner. We had them at the table on Christmas Eve.*

ABOVE RIGHT: *In our brownstone in New York City, Hans and Heidi are baking Christmas cookies. The year is 1970.*

RIGHT: *Our theme tree in 1970 was definitely a child's delight. Heidi adds to the paper tree, decorated with chocolate-covered ginger men, cinnamon stars, popcorn balls, and ice cream cones.*

FAR LEFT, TOP AND BOTTOM: *Here are some of the best reasons we've found for living on a farm—the natural beauty of snow-laden branches, endless vistas, and a stand of birches lining the pasture.* LEFT: *Skitch's 1930 Farmall sits in the field as part of the landscape. We love looking out and seeing it; to us it looks like an old friend.* ABOVE: *We collect pieces of old farm machinery and place them around the property as though they were outdoor sculptures. Through the wheels of an antique hay rake, the 1836 Barn is seen in the distance.* ABOVE RIGHT: *The original sliding doors on either side of our new Silo Gallery barn doors can be closed during severe storms. When that happens, the barn takes back its nineteenth-century look.* RIGHT: *During one winter, McCloud was one of three boarders at our stables who gave our Morgans, Salome and Jupiter, a lot of company.*

A WREATH IS A WREATH IS A WREATH

Round, full, and complete, a wreath is, aside from the tree, our favorite symbol of the season. We've made a lot of them over the years—from dried flowers, vines, herbs, straw, holly, evergreens, and pine cones. They appear all over. A bright green braided soft-sculpture wreath hangs over the wooden playhouse used by Sam and Will. The Peace for All Creatures wreath comes down from the attic and hangs on the door of the 1836 House. Sandra and Hans have a dried wreath with bittersweet for their kitchen door at the Main House.

Wherever there's a door, barn-side, or straight vertical surface, there hangs a wreath to please the eye and delight the heart. Once, we even put one on the stack of Skitch's antique steam engine. Fresh evergreen wreaths come indoors to decorate party buffets, and circles of dried hydrangeas make beautiful centerpieces. A huge green wreath and garland decorated with fruit and red bows hangs high above Skitch when he takes center stage at the New York Pops Christmas concerts at Carnegie Hall.

A wreath, big or small, gives us something during the busy holidays that nothing else does—a kind of reassurance. Like hands reaching, clasping, and completing a circle, the wreath gives simple comfort in a complex time.

TOP LEFT: *On Junie's Hunt Hill Cottage door hangs a straw wreath decorated with ribbon and a replica of her favorite animal—the duck.* TOP MIDDLE: *This life-sized hand-carved knight was commissioned by Skitch years ago as a Christmas present for Ruth. He now stands watch at the entrance to the 1836 Barn holding an oak-leaf-and-berry wreath.* TOP RIGHT: *Our Christmas cactus blooms three times a year but never on Christmas! The sturdy vine wreaths hung outside are decorated with dried flowers and leaves.* MIDDLE RIGHT: *Under evergreen wreaths, two young Silo customers peer out at the barnyard, deep in new-fallen snow.* BOTTOM RIGHT: *From a bounty of dried flowers and herbs comes this wreath for the Main House kitchen door.* BOTTOM LEFT: *A painted-tin ornament of Noah's Ark by Diana Mihaltse tops this wreath and gives it a theme —Peace for All, All Creatures Great and Small!*

OUR ADVENT BREAD WREATH

In the olden days, European families kept track of the time left before Christmas with a traditional living green Advent wreath with four red candles. Before the evening meal on each of the four Sundays before Christmas, someone would refresh the wreath with new boughs and light a new candle. It was a real presence in the house all week long. Each night at dinner, one, two, three, or four candles would burn, depending on how close it was to Christmas.

Over the years, we've seen many variations on the wreath—gold leaf, twisted metal, circles of dried flowers, grapevines, and straw. This year for our wreath we tried something new—a braided golden bread wreath. We baked several in mid-November and froze them. The plan was to have a different edible wreath each Sunday. One by one they would emerge from the freezer, each to be a fresh Advent wreath. But the first wreath looked so good and was such a comforting presence that we didn't want to eat it. It ended up on our breakfast table for the week. We let it dry and used it as a decoration. And so it went with the second, third, and fourth wreaths. All four together in the barn made a wonderful sight. Long after Christmas, Ruth put them in tins to be saved. Perhaps she will lacquer or even paint them for the next season. You can also make one bread wreath, let it dry, lacquer it, and use it for the duration of Advent. If you do, however, be sure to pre-cut the holes for your candles, because once the bread is dry it will crack and break if you try to cut new holes.

This recipe makes two wreaths. Make two separate batches in order to make four wreaths. That way you don't have an unwieldy amount of dough to knead.

1 tablespoon sugar
1 cup warm (105°–110° F.) water
4 packets (¼ ounce each) active dry yeast
3 cups milk, scalded and cooled to 110° F.
3 eggs, lightly beaten
10 cups (approximately) unbleached flour
2 teaspoons salt
1 egg beaten with 1 tablespoon water

Dissolve the sugar in the water in a small mixing bowl. Sprinkle yeast over the surface; stir to dissolve. Let stand until bubbly, about 5 minutes.

Combine the milk and eggs in a large bowl. Stir in the yeast mixture, just enough of the flour (about 7 cups) to make a soft dough, and the salt. Turn the dough out onto a lightly floured board and knead, adding more flour as needed until the dough is smooth and elastic, 10 to 15 minutes. Shape into a ball and place in a lightly greased bowl. Cover bowl with a clean damp towel and place in a warm, draft-free place until doubled in size, about 1 hour.

Punch the dough down and divide in half. Divide each half into thirds and shape each third into a ball. Set aside and let rest 10 minutes.

Preheat the oven to 375° F.

On a lightly floured surface, use your hands to roll each ball into a strand 36 inches long. Braid 3 strands into a rope and shape the rope to form a circle. Pinch to seal the ends and place on a lightly greased baking sheet. Brush generously with egg wash. Bake until golden brown, about 35 to 40 minutes. *Makes 2 wreaths, each 13 inches in diameter.*

❧ ❧

RIGHT: *When we make wreaths of bread we count on each one having its own unique shape. No two will be alike—one fat, one thin, one lopsided. Each will have character.*

First Week of Advent

A NATIVE AMERICAN FEAST

We have always been moved by Native American art, and have in the past been inclined to assume that the art we liked was done by the Indians of the Southwest or the Great Plains. Only recently, through a show at the Silo Gallery, did we learn of the wealth of Indian art and tradition here in our own Connecticut backyard, there being six active Algonquin tribes still living here as our neighbors. The Schaghticoke are the nearest, just a few miles away in Kent.

◆19◆

Wild Mushroom Caviar

Algonquin Pumpkin Peanut Soup with Spicy Gingered Yogurt

Plum Raisin Bread with Cranberry Maple Butter

Delaware Crab Cakes with Chimichuri Sauce

Connecticut Mohegan Succotash

Wild Rice with Roasted Hazelnuts and Pecans

Maple Nut Flan

FAR LEFT: *Wooden flatware and napkins are arranged in a birchbark tray. Green wheat in natural-looking flower-bulb vases and a string of cranberries add color to this buffet table.*

LEFT: *Dried corn in the husk borders narrow wooden crates full of a variety of chips for the party.*

Our gallery director and curator, Peter Dubos, featured Native American art from all over the country but paid special attention to the art and customs of the Algonquin tribes that live near New Milford, including the work of Schaghticoke carver and craftsman Butch Lydem and traditional storyteller Trudie Lamb Richmond.

A whole world of Northeastern Indian art, history, food, and traditions not only opened up to us but opened us up at the same time. We learned so much about the artisans, farmers, and hunters who settled here long before any Europeans that we wanted to share some of it with our friends. What better way than with a feast inspired by the foods enjoyed for centuries by Native Americans?

BELOW: *Our old English tavern table and a wicker cocktail table lend rustic texture and color to the feast.*

LEFT: *Dried pomegranates and painted dried gourds are nestled into a grapevine basket for decoration.*

We hosted this first Advent meal, since it was unseasonably warm, outside in the tobacco barn, where we were surrounded by all the things we gather from the farm for drying—hydrangeas, wheat grasses, wild barley, pine cones, flowers. A bare silver birch tree, cut from the thick woods at the top of the farm, stood as a symbol of the end of fall and the coming of Christmas. We decorated it with Native American ornaments—dream catchers and talking sticks handmade by Dale Carson, a local artist of Abkenaki Pennacook descent, and ornaments inspired by Indians of the Southwest, Northwest, and the Plains. Bales of straw surrounded the tree and a wood-plank table held the buffet.

The food was chosen with the help of our neighbor, Barrie Kavasch, a renowned food historian and author of *Native Harvests: Recipes and Botanicals of the American Indians.* We served it all in bowls and containers handcrafted by Barbara Eigen. She's an artist whose work we have collected for years because all of it is inspired by nature.

It was an exciting way to begin our Advent season—with new ideas and traditions from a very old culture. We have added them to our own now, to have for years to come. We lit the first candle in our Advent wreath and invited our friends to enjoy a delicious feast.

◆ 21 ◆

WILD MUSHROOM CAVIAR

Members of the Connecticut Indian tribes near here are expert wild-mushroom gatherers. And when Ruth was young, every child in her region was taught how to recognize and collect edible mushrooms in the forest. However, now we do most of our gathering at the supermarket!

3–4 pounds select fresh wild mushrooms (store-bought cultivated mushrooms can also be used), or about 2 ounces dried mushrooms for each 1 pound fresh

½ cup corn or sunflower-seed oil

2 cups diced onions (about 2 large)

½ cup finely chopped fresh parsley

½ cup finely diced garlic (about 8 cloves)

½ cup finely chopped whole scallions

3 tablespoons Worcestershire sauce

¼ teaspoon hot-pepper sauce

1 tablespoon fresh lemon juice

¼ teaspoon salt

½ teaspoon freshly ground pepper

¼ teaspoon paprika

Wipe (do not wash) the mushrooms clean of any dirt. Remove any woody stems. Chop fine and set aside.

If you're using dried mushrooms, place them in a bowl and add enough hot water to cover. Soak until softened, 1 to 4 hours. Drain, reserving liquid for use at another time in soups, stews, or sauces. Remove any woody stems and chop fine.

Heat the oil in a large heavy skillet over medium heat until hot but not smoking. Add the onions; cook 2 minutes. Stir in the parsley, garlic, and scallions; continue cooking until a good fragrance develops, about 6 to 10 minutes. Add remaining ingredients and stir thoroughly. Serve hot or at room temperature. *Makes about 6 cups.*

🙚 🙜

ALGONQUIN PUMPKIN PEANUT SOUP WITH SPICY GINGERED YOGURT

The name Algonquin refers to all Indians that spoke Algonquian, the language that bonded so many of the small tribes of the Northeast. These tribes were the main inhabitants of New England for centuries. They prepared and ate a coarse version of this smooth and creamy soup.

¼ cup sunflower-seed oil
½ cup finely chopped whole scallions
1 teaspoon finely diced garlic (about 1 small clove)
3 tablespoons finely chopped fresh ginger root
½ cup shelled, skinned peanuts
2 quarts milk, scalded and cooled to 110° F.
3 pounds puree of cooked sugar pumpkin (about 1 small sugar pumpkin)
3 tablespoons unsalted butter, cut into bits
½ teaspoon salt
½ teaspoon ground cloves
¼ teaspoon freshly grated nutmeg, plus more for garnish
½ cup honey
Spicy Gingered Yogurt (recipe follows)

Heat the oil in a large heavy skillet over medium heat. Reduce heat to low and add the scallions; cook 1 minute. Add the garlic, ginger, and peanuts. Continue cooking until the scallions are soft, about 5 minutes. Place the mixture in the container of a blender or food processor and process until nearly smooth. Set aside.

Combine the scalded milk, pumpkin, butter, salt, cloves, nutmeg, and honey in a large saucepan or soup pot. Slowly heat to a gentle boil, stirring constantly. Add the reserved pureed ingredients and simmer another 5 minutes.

Serve hot, at room temperature, or cold. La-dle into individual bowls and top with a dollop of Spicy Gingered Yogurt and a sprinkle of freshly grated nutmeg. *Serves 16.*

SPICY GINGERED YOGURT

1 tablespoon unsalted butter
1 tablespoon finely diced fresh ginger root or crystallized ginger
1 cup plain, lemon, or vanilla yogurt

Melt the butter in a small skillet over medium heat. Add the ginger and cook until softened. Cool.

Combine the ginger and yogurt in a small bowl; stir until well blended. Chill. *Makes 1 cup.*

◆ 23 ◆

ABOVE: *To serve the soup hot as can be, we preheat these pumpkin-shaped ceramic bowls and tureen.*

PLUM RAISIN BREAD WITH CRANBERRY MAPLE BUTTER

Our friend Barrie Kavasch, who was the curator of a traveling exhibit for the Smithsonian called "Native Harvests: Plants in American Indian Life," tells us it's common for Indians from the Pacific to the Atlantic coasts to harvest wild foods that grow close to home. Most of us are limited by what is offered in the supermarket, but hundreds of wild nuts and fruits thrive on bushes, trees, and vines all over the country and never make it to local produce sections. Uncultivated hazelnuts and wild plums are just two examples. Only a few people still know how to recognize and harvest them; this recipe is inspired by their expertise.

1 cup seedless raisins or currants

1 cup hazelnuts, toasted and chopped

4 cups sifted flour

3 teaspoons baking soda

1 ½ teaspoons cinnamon

1 ½ teaspoons salt (optional)

1 teaspoon ground cloves

1 can (16 ½ ounces) purple plums

1 cup (2 sticks) unsalted butter, melted

1 cup honey

½ cup maple syrup

Cranberry Maple Butter (recipe follows)

Place the raisins in a small bowl and add 1 cup hot water to cover. Let soak 30 minutes.

Preheat the oven to 350° F. Grease and flour two 5x9-inch loaf pans.

Combine the nuts, flour, baking soda, cinnamon, salt, and cloves in a large mixing bowl. Set aside.

Drain the plum juice and reserve for use in the Cranberry Maple Butter. Remove the plum pits and mash the fruit in a medium bowl. Add the raisins with their soaking water, butter, honey, and maple syrup. Stir until well combined. Gradually add this mixture to the dry ingredients, stirring well after each addition.

Pour the batter into the prepared pans. Bake until a toothpick inserted in the center comes out clean, about 60 minutes. (Since batters made with honey and maple syrup tend to burn, watch bread carefully and cover with foil if it browns too quickly.)

Cool in pans on a wire rack for 10 minutes. Loosen the sides with a knife, unmold, and cool the breads completely on a rack. Slice and serve with Cranberry Maple Butter. *Makes 2 loaves.*

ABOVE: *Guests help themselves to crab cakes, wild rice, succotash, and Plum Raisin Bread with Cranberry Maple Butter.*
RIGHT: *Clay baskets, handcrafted by New York designer Rina Peleg, are filled with spiced popcorn and placed on straw bales next to bundles of birch logs, which we will give to friends who have fireplaces.*

CRANBERRY MAPLE BUTTER

Ruth never tasted cranberries before moving to America, and she hasn't stopped finding ways to use them since. We're happy to find out that the Narragansett and the Wampanoag tribes still own, plant, and harvest some of the great cranberry bogs in Massachusetts.

1 package (12 ounces) fresh cranberries, washed and
*   picked over*
½ cup maple syrup
½ cup sugar
1 cup plum juice (reserved from Plum Raisin Bread
*   recipe) or water*
2 tablespoons cornstarch
2 tablespoons cold water

Combine cranberries, maple syrup, sugar, and reserved plum juice in a medium saucepan. Heat to boiling. Reduce heat and simmer, covered, until slightly thickened, about 45 minutes.

Dissolve the cornstarch in the 2 tablespoons cold water in a small bowl. Heat the cranberry mixture to a rolling boil and whisk in the cornstarch mixture. Remove from heat. When mixture is cool, puree in a food processor or blender until smooth. *Serves 16. Makes 1½ to 2 cups.*

↭

John Finnegan's Popcorn

The chef de cuisine at Gail's Station House in Ridgefield, Connecticut, and his wife, Patty, helped us prepare the food for this party. We surprised John with a last-minute request to come up with a recipe for flavored popcorn. After all, the American Indians invented popcorn!

AROMATIC SPICE POPCORN

½ cup walnut oil
1 tablespoon brown sugar
1 tablespoon coarse salt
1 teaspoon minced garlic (about 1 clove)
1 teaspoon cumin
¼ cup finely chopped whole scallion
8 ounces popcorn, unpopped

Combine walnut oil, brown sugar, salt, garlic, cumin, and scallion in a small saucepan. Heat to warm through and to dissolve the sugar. Set aside to cool 10 minutes.

Pop the corn and place in a large bowl. Gradually add the spice mixture to the corn, tossing well until corn is coated. *Makes 6 quarts.*

SWEET AND SOUR GLAZED POPCORN

2 tablespoons balsamic vinegar
⅓ cup maple syrup
1 cup pecans, chopped and toasted
¼ cup shelled and skinned peanuts
¼ cup golden raisins
8 ounces popcorn, unpopped

Combine the vinegar, maple syrup, pecans, peanuts, and raisins. Let stand 15 minutes.

Pop the corn and place in a large bowl. Gradually add the sweet and sour mixture, tossing until corn is well coated. *Makes 6 quarts.*

DELAWARE CRAB CAKES WITH CHIMICHURI SAUCE

This recipe honors the Algonquins who fished the Northeast coastal waters. Don't skip making the Chimichuri Sauce. Forms of this name, derived originally from the Peruvian, have come to mean "relish" or "salsa" in many South American Indian languages. Even though it's more South American than North, its spiciness opens your taste buds and brings out the flavor of the crab wonderfully.

½ cup sunflower-seed oil
¼ cup finely chopped onions (about 1 small)
¾ cup finely chopped fresh parsley
1 ¾ cups fine yellow cornmeal
6 cups flaked crabmeat (about 6 6-ounce cans), drained
1 cup finely diced celery (about 2 stalks)
¼ cup fresh lemon juice
½ teaspoon salt (optional)
¾ teaspoon paprika
¼ teaspoon white pepper
¼ cup finely chopped fresh dill
6 eggs, lightly beaten
½ cup chicken stock
1 cup corn oil
2 bunches scallions for garnish (optional)
Chimichuri Sauce (recipe follows)

Heat the sunflower-seed oil in a medium skillet over medium heat until hot. Add the onion; cook 1 minute. Add ¼ cup of the parsley and ¼ cup of the cornmeal and continue cooking, stirring often, for 5 minutes. Set aside until cool.

Combine the onion mixture, crabmeat, celery, remaining parsley, lemon juice, salt, ½ teaspoon paprika, pepper, all but 1 teaspoon of the dill, eggs, chicken stock, and ½ cup of the remaining cornmeal. Stir until well combined. Cover and chill for 2 to 3 hours.

Combine the remaining cornmeal, dill, and paprika in a shallow bowl. Divide the crab mixture into 16 equal portions. Shape each into a cake about 3½ inches in diameter and dust lightly with the cornmeal mixture.

Heat the corn oil in a large skillet over medium-high heat until hot. Add the cakes a few at a time, cooking until golden on both sides, about 15 minutes. Cover with foil and keep warm in a low oven until all cakes are browned. Serve hot, garnished with scallions if desired, and pass the Chimichuri Sauce on the side. *Serves 16.*

CHIMICHURI SAUCE

½ cup finely chopped fresh parsley
½ cup finely chopped fresh cilantro
½ cup minced onions (about 1 large)
¼ cup minced garlic (about 4 large cloves)
1 ½ teaspoons finely chopped fresh oregano
¼ cup balsamic vinegar
¼ cup red-wine vinegar
1 teaspoon cayenne pepper (or less or more to taste)
Salt and freshly ground pepper to taste
Approximately ½ cup olive oil

Combine the parsley, cilantro, onion, minced garlic, oregano, and vinegars in a medium glass or ceramic bowl. Stir in the cayenne, salt, and pepper. Set aside 10 minutes at room temperature to allow flavors to develop. Add enough oil to cover the mixture and serve, or cover and refrigerate overnight. *Makes about 2 cups.*

CONNECTICUT MOHEGAN SUCCOTASH

Courtland Fowler was an elder among the Connecticut Mohegans when he gave this recipe to Barrie Kavasch years ago. He had re-created it in detail from his memory of his grandmother's cooking. We thank Barrie for passing it on to us. It's a perfect mix of fresh corn, beans, and squash, and it's the first succotash Skitch has ever liked!

½ cup sunflower-seed oil

1 cup finely chopped onions (about 2 large)

¼ cup finely chopped garlic (about 8–10 cloves)

1 teaspoon freshly ground pepper

½ teaspoon paprika

10 ears fresh corn, cut into 2-inch pieces

2 2-pound packages frozen baby lima beans

1 medium yellow squash, cubed

1 medium zucchini, cubed

1 red bell pepper, roasted, peeled, seeded, and cut into long strips

1 green bell pepper, roasted, peeled, seeded, and cut into cubes or triangles

3 cups chicken stock or water

Salt

½ cup finely chopped whole scallions

½ cup finely chopped fresh parsley

ABOVE: *Egyptian onions instead of scallions decorate the platter of crab cakes. This variety grows easily in our garden and provides us with this unusual wild-looking garnish.*

Heat the oil in a large lidded heavy saucepan or soup pot over medium heat until hot. Add the onion; cook one minute. Add the garlic and cook until the onion is soft, about 5 minutes. Stir in the pepper and paprika and remove from heat.

Combine the corn, lima beans, squash, zucchini, and bell peppers in the saucepan. Add the stock or water and heat to boiling, stirring occasionally. Reduce heat, cover, and simmer gently 15 minutes. Remove from heat. Add salt to taste. Stir in the scallions and parsley and let stand, covered, 5 minutes.

Ladle into large bowls and serve. *Serves 16.*

WILD RICE WITH ROASTED HAZELNUTS AND PECANS

Wild rice and hazelnuts grow very well without any help from farmers. The Indians included both in their cooking. We added the pecans to bring in a southern taste.

8 cups water
Salt
½ cup maple syrup
4 cups wild rice
½ cup sunflower-seed oil
½ cup finely chopped whole scallions
½ cup hazelnuts, roughly chopped and toasted
½ cup pecan pieces, toasted

Place the water in a large saucepan, add the salt to taste, and heat to boiling. Add the maple syrup, then sprinkle the rice over the water. Reduce heat to medium-low, cover, and simmer gently until the rice is tender, about 45 minutes.

Meanwhile, heat ¼ cup of the oil in a small skillet over medium heat. Add the scallions and cook 2 minutes.

When the rice is tender, remove from heat. Add the scallions, nuts, and remaining oil. Stir well. Serve hot, at room temperature, or chilled. *Serves 16.*

❦❧

LEFT: *The feast is spread before us: Algonquin Pumpkin Peanut Soup, Wild Mushroom Caviar, Wild Rice with Roasted Hazelnuts and Pecans, Delaware Crab Cakes, and Connecticut Mohegan Succotash.*

FAR RIGHT: *Barbara Eigen's maple-leaf plates differ from each other in color, just as maple leaves in nature do.*

MAPLE NUT FLAN

Ground-up nuts and maple syrup add an Algonquin touch to what is actually a Hispanic sweet custard. Skitch loves flan, and this rendition has become one of our family's favorites.

1 ½ cups maple syrup
3 cups sugar
1 cup hazelnuts
2 ½ cups milk
1 tablespoon vanilla extract
6 eggs, lightly beaten
4 eggs, separated
Zest of 2 lemons for garnish (optional)
Crème de cassis (optional)
Steamed cranberries for garnish (optional)

Preheat the oven to 325° F.

Heat the syrup and 1 cup of the sugar in a large heavy skillet over medium heat. Stir constantly with a wooden spoon until syrup thickens and turns dark, about 15 minutes. Pour into an 8-inch round glass mold, or divide among individual custard cups, tipping and turning mold or cups until the entire bottom is covered. Set aside to cool.

Blanch the hazelnuts in boiling water 5 minutes. Drain and place in the container of a food processor or blender. Process just until pureed. Set aside.

Combine the milk, remaining sugar, and vanilla extract in a medium saucepan. Heat to boiling; reduce heat and simmer over medium heat until mixture reduces by ⅓. Remove from heat and cool slightly.

Beat the 6 whole eggs and the 4 yolks in a large bowl. In another bowl, beat the 4 egg whites until stiff but not dry. Gradually whisk the yolk mixture into the cooled milk mixture. Fold in the

egg whites and the hazelnut puree. Pour into the prepared mold, or divide among the custard cups, and place the mold or cups in a larger pan filled with hot water that comes halfway up the side of the mold or cups. Bake until a toothpick inserted in the center comes out clean, about 1 ½ hours. Cool, then chill at least 4 hours.

To unmold and serve, dip bottom and sides of the mold or custard cups into hot water for a few seconds. Loosen the sides with a sharp knife and invert onto a serving plate. Garnish with optional zest, cassis, or cranberries to please your palate and your eye. *Serves 16.*

৵৶

LIVE AND LET DRY

You name it—we dry it! We love to give anything that has grown and adorned the farm a second life. We harvest hydrangeas yearly and keep baskets full of dried blooms forever, it seems. There are scientific and precise methods for drying flowers, leaves, and vegetables, but we let things dry naturally without much help from the experts—sometimes inadvertently leaving a lemon in a wooden bowl until it's dry. And more than once, we've left a butternut squash used as a centerpiece from Thanksgiving on a sideboard and forgotten about it. Then the day comes when we finally notice it and are delighted by its transformation into a bright gourd.

Drying flowers and other growing things is a simple and natural process. If protected from moisture, these things will dry on their own. Have you ever received a bouquet of roses or a basket of mixed flowers and not added extra water because you were leaving town? Sometimes, weeks later, when you returned, did you find that the roses had dried beautifully? That's when you can take the roses out of the vase, tie them with a velvet ribbon, and lay them casually on a side table. Or have you ever come home after vacation to a fall flower basket in which some blooms have dried beautifully and others have not? Pull out the good-looking flowers and make a smaller arrangement to tie with a ribbon to add to a present or to fill a small basket.

Most of the time, however, we collect flowers and plants from our gardens and hillsides and dry them intentionally. It takes three to

FAR LEFT: *Thistles, dried herbs, branches, leaves, and flowers come out of the tobacco barn to the porch, where Ruth takes stock and gathers inspiration for making wreaths and decorations.*

ABOVE: *We buy artichokes and pomegranates for drying by the dozen.* BELOW: *White hydrangeas turn caramel-colored when dried.* BOTTOM: *Most of this early-Christmas bouquet from Bobbie and Peter Lane dried beautifully.*

four weeks to give most plants and vegetables a good drying. So when planning for Christmas-gift giving, start at least one month ahead. Thanksgiving is a good time to collect gourds, squashes, artichokes, and pomegranates, which will make excellent fresh decorations for this holiday feast. Afterward, spread them out on a wooden rack or window screen, place them in a wire basket or colander, or stand them up in small juice glasses and turn them frequently while they dry.

Dried artichokes make beautiful candle holders and centerpieces. It takes about three weeks for them to dry. For trouble-free drying, place them upright in narrow cups or small juice glasses so that the air circulates all around. When they are completely dry, you can remove the center core with a sharp knife or scissors if you want to make them into candle holders, or simply place them whole in a bowl with pine cones and dried flowers. Spray them silver or gold if you like by placing a few dried artichokes in a large paper bag. Spray paint into the bag a few seconds, then shake the bag to turn the artichokes. Keep spraying and shaking until the artichokes are completely coated.

Pomegranates, too, take about three weeks to dry, using the same method as with the artichokes. Make sure they are thoroughly dry before painting, and paint using the same method as used for the artichokes.

We also spray-paint apples and pears. Fruit, however, need not be dried in order to be sprayed. Bowls of golden pears and silver apples will last three to four weeks. Tiny lady apples can be sprayed and hung as ornaments.

Herbs like rosemary, thyme, and bay leaf, as well as flowers and flowering bushes like hydrangeas, must be harvested at their peak, preferably on a sunny day after at least one dry day, so that you start out with as little moisture as possible. For hydrangeas, wait until all the little blossoms are wide open and almost ready to lose color. Cut as long a stem as possible and strip most of the leaves, leaving just

one or two nearest the blossom. Bundle them into bunches of four to eight and fasten with a rubber band or twine. We hang them upside down in the living room for decoration as they dry, and give them in bouquets as gifts.

You can also place hydrangeas and other long-stemmed flowers loosely in a tall crock or vase and let them dry standing up. Do the same with wild grasses, thistles, wheat, barley, cornstalks, branches of brightly colored fall leaves, and bittersweet. These make beautiful arrangements or wreaths to decorate your home, a corner table, or an entryway. Little sprigs of them look wonderful tied in a bunch to a gift package. Leafless branches and driftwood, too, can become centerpieces or decorations for an entryway when hung with special ornaments.

We collect pine cones every year, adding more and more to the bags of them in the attic. The best time for collecting is after a few days of dry weather, when the cones have fallen and dried on the ground. The few that may still be sticky with resin will dry out at home in five or six days. Pine cones can be tied to packages or piled in bowls just for the fun of looking at them. We've also attached them to round or tree-shaped wire forms to make wreaths or trees. We pile them under the Christmas tree instead of wrapping the tree with a skirt.

Save your candle stubs throughout the year. Melt them down and dip pine cones in the liquid wax until they are completely covered. Let them dry on wax paper until set. Bundle them up in a sack with ribbon and give them to a fireplace friend—one who loves building fires indoors—or use them yourself. The waxed pine cones are terrific fire starters. Three or four will provide enough tinder to start a blazing fire.

TOP: *Dried pomegranates are stored in this old market basket until we find places for them in bowls and on other decorations.* ABOVE: *The painting by Cookie Finn, the found-metal sculpture by Bill Heise, and the Santa Fe cabinet create a triple-cow setting for the big Red Delicious apples ready for spraying.*

Gifts That Grow

So many of our friends appreciate a simple growing gift. Paperwhites about to bloom, potted amaryllis, or hyacinths are wonderful presents to give and they can be started from ordinary bulbs. Choose an interesting crock to hold the bulbs—a French mustard jar and water, a pottery bowl filled with marble chips and water, a cup with a saucer, a mug, or a bulb vase with water. The container will be an extra gift long after the flowers have gone.

Start the bulbs early. Paperwhites need about three weeks to bloom. The amaryllis needs five weeks. Cover them in their containers with small bags to give them darkness until they start growing. Place them where they will be undisturbed. Soon they will sprout roots. Then they'll send stems shooting up and you'll take the bags off to watch them grow. By Christmas Day, there'll be flowers for you and for gifts.

We start dozens of paperwhites and hyacinths early. Then we start more a couple of weeks later, then more in another week, so that we are assured of flowers in the house all winter long.

We buy our bulbs from White Flower Farm in Connecticut.

LEFT: *If placed in bowls three weeks ahead, paperwhites will be blossoming by Christmas—just in time for gift-giving. We tied these with raffia and attached Mexican tin ornaments.*

RIGHT: *A blooming hyacinth in a country crock is a gift that always produces a smile.*

GIFTS FOR THE PANTRY

❧ ❧

We love pantry foods, and we like having lots of canned goods ready to use on the pantry shelves (probably the reason we own a store). Our pantry at home begins to fill up in August. Eventually, there are dozens of large and small jars of put-ups from the garden—peppers, onions, green beans, tomatoes, mixed vegetables, and fruit butters from the bounty of nearby orchards.

A gift from your pantry for another's is a great present. People like to receive homemade condiments, and they love good-looking old-fashioned clear containers, packed with red and green vegetables, translucent herbed vinegars and oils, or colorful dried pasta. At our house, a tall two-quart French canning jar, layered with green beans, wax beans, carrots, shallots, and red peppers, sat outside the pantry for years. It moved around, sometimes sitting on a sideboard, sometimes on a windowsill. We just liked looking at it—we didn't want to open it and have to lose it. One day, a house guest unwittingly opened the jar and helped himself. The vegetables were delicious but our romance with the beautiful jar was ended.

We use reliable canning jars that give a good seal, and we process all fruit and pickled foods in a water bath to ensure that the gift won't spoil. Always label your pantry goods. Even if you think you won't forget what it is and when you canned it, you will. Give it a name and a date.

The French canning jars are our favorites because long after the contents are gone, the beautiful jar, with its unique metal-hinged glass top, makes a wonderful container. They always have a good second life.

Pear Chutney

Hot Honey Mustard

Basil Vinegar

Rosemary Olive Oil

Pickled Peppers and Onions

Baby Carrots and Cauliflower

Mixed Garden Vegetables

❖ 37 ❖

FAR LEFT: *Ruth lines up jars of pantry gifts on the sill above her desk. She loves looking at them while she decides who will get what.*

Pear Chutney

Don't expect hot and spicy here. This is a mild condiment for accompanying savory or distinctive-tasting meats, like smoked ham or turkey.

5 pounds ripe pears, peeled, cored, and diced
2 lemons, thinly sliced
1 cup seedless golden raisins
½ cup crystallized ginger, finely chopped
1 cup cider vinegar
1 cup brown sugar
½ teaspoon freshly grated nutmeg
1 teaspoon mustard seed
1 cup fresh cranberries, washed and picked over
2 teaspoons cornstarch
2 tablespoons water

Combine pears, lemons, raisins, ginger, vinegar, brown sugar, nutmeg, and mustard seed in a large saucepan. Heat to boiling; reduce heat and simmer, uncovered, 20 minutes. Add cranberries and simmer 5 minutes more. Dissolve the cornstarch in the water and add to fruit mixture. Cook until thickened, about 2–3 minutes. Pour into three hot sterilized pint jars, leaving ¼-inch space at the top. Seal jars and place vertically in a large pot filled with gently boiling water. The tops of the jars must be at least 1 inch under water. Simmer gently at least 15 minutes. Cool and store in a cool dry place. *Makes 3 pints.*

Hot Honey Mustard

This is for serious mustard lovers, not for the kids and their hot dogs.

1 cup honey
2¼ cups dry mustard
3 cups cider vinegar
9 medium eggs
3 tablespoons green peppercorns in brine, drained
    (optional)

Combine all ingredients except peppercorns in the top of a double boiler. Heat over gently boiling water, whisking constantly, until thick and smooth, about 10 minutes. Add peppercorns if desired and pour into six hot sterilized ½-pint jars, leaving ¼ inch at the top. Seal jars and place vertically in a large pot filled with gently boiling water. The tops of the jars must be at least 1 inch under water. Simmer gently 10 minutes. Cool and store in a cool place. *Makes 6 half pints.*

Variation: Herb Mustard

Add 1 tablespoon chopped fresh dill, 1 tablespoon chopped fresh basil, and 1 tablespoon chopped fresh thyme to mustard before bottling.

ABOVE RIGHT: *It's hard to give herbed oils and vinegars away when they look so at home on the windowsill. We often, though, simply hand one to a dinner guest as he leaves.*

FAR RIGHT: *An old toy horse that usually sits on the sill moves down to the desk while Ruth makes her gift lists.*

LEFT: *From the window, we see the shadow of an evergreen tree and our chimney.*

ROSEMARY OLIVE OIL

Another beautiful-to-look-at, delightful-to-use gift for the cook in your life. If your oil clouds a bit, don't worry: it probably means you're keeping it too cool. Moving it to a warmer part of the room will usually clear it up.

3 sprigs fresh rosemary, washed and patted dry
1 clove garlic, peeled
1 whole dried red pepper
1 teaspoon multicolored peppercorns (red, green, and
    black)
1 quart olive oil

Insert the rosemary, garlic, pepper, and peppercorns in a sterilized 1-quart or larger bottle fitted with a cork or stopper. Heat the oil in a saucepan until just warmed through. Using a funnel, pour the oil into the bottle, leaving ¼ inch at the top. Seal and store in a moderately cool place for 1 month while flavors develop. *Makes 1 quart.*

ৡৱ

BASIL VINEGAR

We keep a bottle of this on the windowsill. It's as beautiful to look at as it is delicious.

3 sprigs fresh opal basil, washed and patted dry
1 quart red-wine vinegar

Cut off the tough basil stems and insert leaves and tender stems into a clean 1-quart bottle fitted with a cork or stopper. Heat the vinegar in a saucepan until just warmed through. Using a funnel, pour warm vinegar into the bottle, leaving ¼ inch at the top. Seal and store in a cool place. It takes about 10 days for the flavor to develop. *Makes 1 quart.*

ৡৱ

PICKLED PEPPERS AND ONIONS

12 red, green, and yellow bell peppers (4 each), seeded
*   and quartered*
4 medium onions, peeled and cut into eighths
4 sprigs fresh basil, washed and patted dry
2 jalapeño peppers, quartered and seeded
4 teaspoons mustard seed
2 quarts warm Pickling Liquid (recipe follows)

Blanch the peppers and onions in boiling water 1 minute, then drain and pat dry. Divide evenly between 2 sterilized 1-quart jars and pack very tightly. Divide the basil, jalapeño, and mustard seed and add to each jar. Add pickling liquid, leaving ¼ inch at the top of each jar. (Refrigerate any leftover pickling liquid.) Insert a non-metallic spoon down the sides of the jar to remove air bubbles. Seal jars and place vertically in a large pot filled with gently boiling water. The tops of the jars must be at least 1 inch under water. Simmer gently at least 20 minutes. Cool and store in a cool dry place. *Makes 2 quarts.*

PICKLING LIQUID

Use a light vinegar for light vegetables, a dark cider vinegar for darker vegetables. Pickling salt is a fine-grain salt with no additives or preservatives. If you can't find it, substitute the coarser kosher salt, which is also made without additives.

5¼ cups white or cider vinegar (5% acidity)
1¾ cups sugar
1½ cups water
¼ cup pickling or kosher salt

Combine all ingredients in a large saucepan. Heat to boiling and cool until warm, then use as directed in recipe. *Makes about 2 quarts.*

❧ ❧

BABY CARROTS AND CAULIFLOWER

1½ pounds baby carrots, peeled and trimmed (leave ¼
*   inch of top greens)*
¾ pound cauliflower, washed and separated into florets
12 sprigs fresh marjoram or 3 teaspoons dried marjoram
2 quarts warm Pickling Liquid (see recipe at left)

Blanch the vegetables in boiling water 1 minute, then drain and pat dry. Pack tightly into a sterilized 1-pint jar. Add the marjoram and pickling liquid, leaving ¼ inch at the top (Refrigerate any leftover pickling liquid.) Insert a non-metallic spoon down the sides of the jar to remove air bubbles. Seal the jar and place vertically in a large pot filled with gently boiling water. The top of the jar must be at least 1 inch under water. Simmer gently at least 15 minutes. Cool and store in a cool dry place. *Makes 3 pints.*

❧ ❧

Mixed Garden Vegetables

1 medium head cauliflower, washed and separated into
 florets

1 medium bunch carrots, peeled and cut into ¼-inch
 slices

2 large red bell peppers, seeded and cut into eighths

2 large green bell peppers, seeded and cut into eighths

2 large yellow bell peppers, seeded and cut into eighths

1 pound green beans, trimmed and washed

1 pound wax beans, trimmed and washed

1 pound shallots (about 4 dozen), peeled

8 cloves garlic, peeled

8 jalapeño peppers

8 sprigs fresh lovage or celery leaves

2 teaspoons mustard seed

2 teaspoons multicolored peppercorns (red, green, and
 black)

About 2 quarts warm Pickling Liquid (see recipe, page 40

Blanch the cauliflower, carrots, peppers, and
beans in boiling water 3 minutes, then drain and
pat dry. Divide the shallots evenly between two
sterilized 1.5-liter French canning jars and pack
into a neat layer at the bottom of each jar. Layer
the remaining blanched vegetables on top of the
shallots in any order you like. Add the garlic,
jalapeño peppers, lovage, mustard seed, and peppercorns as you go along. Pack the jars very tightly.
Add the pickling liquid, leaving ¼ inch at the top
of each jar. Insert a nonmetallic spoon down the
sides of the jars to remove air bubbles. Seal the jars
and place vertically in a large pot filled with gently
boiling water. The tops of the jars must be at least
1 inch under water. Simmer gently at least 20 minutes. Cool and store in a cool dry place. *Makes 3
liters.*

ೊ ೂ

LEFT: *As seen from the outside, the original barn window
frames some of our dried herbs and jars of pantry giveaways.*

Quick Pantry Presents

These are quick only because they don't require
processing in a hot-water bath. Nor does the jar
or container need to have a perfect seal—you can
safely pack these in antique jars, crocks, and containers if you want to.

Vanilla Sugar This is so simple and yet such a
welcome gift.

Place a whole vanilla bean in a decorative jar
or crock (about 6 inches high and 2¼ inches in
diameter) filled with granulated white sugar or
turbinado sugar. Set aside for at least 2 weeks
(the longer the better) while the vanilla flavors
the sugar. You may refill the crock with sugar
three times without replacing the bean.

Clove Sugar Follow same directions as above
but substitute 12 cloves for the vanilla bean.

Dried Fruit A mixture of apple slices, pears,
apricots, prunes, or figs layered in a French canning jar makes a beautiful gift.

Nuts Give a large glass crock filled with un-
shelled mixed nuts. Attach a nutcracker.

Dried Foods Fill any jar with someone's favorite
spice, pasta, or layers of different-colored beans.

Spices Fill a small, corked jar with whole nutmeg. Tie a grater to it with a red string.

Fill a small corked jar with multicolored
peppercorns and give with a pepper mill.

Spiced Salt Mix dried herbs, pepper, salt, and
dried lemon peel in an attractive glass container.
Package your salt in a decorative jar and design
your own label.

SURPRISE GIFTS FROM GEORGE COTHRAN'S FARM IN PUERTO RICO

S ome of the biggest pleasures of the season are the surprises—the unexpected visits, long-distance telephone calls, and packages from old friends. George Cothran was a business partner of ours in the early days. He now owns a farm in Puerto Rico. When our daughter, Heidi, returned from a December visit there, George sent her back to us laden with gifts—fresh pineapple, a hand of bananas, raw sugar, bottles of cinnamon syrup, and jars of canned fruit. We immediately turned his gifts into a luscious lunch.

FAR LEFT: *These pineapples were harvested the day before we ate them. When we cut them open, the tropical aroma filled the 1836 Barn.*

◆43◆

SMITHFIELD HAM WITH FRESH PINEAPPLE AND SWEET FRIED PLANTAINS

2 fresh pineapples
2 tablespoons unsalted butter
⅓ cup turbinado sugar or light brown sugar
8 small whole sweet plantains or bananas, peeled
3 pounds Smithfield or any smoked and cured ham, sliced

Cut the pineapple into quarters and slice off the woody core. (We left the stem and feathery leaves because of the great look.) Melt the butter in a large skillet over medium heat. Add the sugar; stir until sugar is dissolved and mixture is syrupy. Add plantains and cook, turning with tongs, until brown, about 2–3 minutes.

Serve with ham and eat the pineapple as you would a wedge of watermelon—with your hands. *Serves 4.*

SAINT NICHOLAS DAY

◈◈

When we were children, there were some traditions we observed during the holidays that have since faded. Ruth vividly remembers Saint Nicholas Day, December 6—all children made a wish list and placed it in one of their shoes on the evening before. Then they placed their shoes outside the bedroom door or at the foot of the bed. During the night, they hoped, Saint Nicholas would come and pick up the wish list. They left some sweet and savory refreshment for the saint. In the morning, if the list was gone and a candy was in the shoe, the children knew Saint Nicholas approved of the list and could do something to grant the wishes. If the list was gone but there was a rock or switch in the shoe, the children knew they had to shape up a bit.

Now, at the farm, Saint Nicholas Day has become an occasion to gather with friends who have long-standing handwork projects to finish. Ruth has been working on a rug for fifteen years! But it no longer seems to matter whether these projects get finished—at least not this year. What matters is that we gather with friends, to visit, work, and eat.

This is a good "after" party—after ornament making, decorating, or wrapping packages—and it makes a good office celebration. It can all be made the day ahead. The individual cheeses look so festive and taste good hot or at room temperature. Each of the small cheese rounds was wrapped in phyllo dough, a Greek pastry readily available in most supermarkets. We baked three each of four different styles, all with Camembert, but you can choose your own cheese or assemble a variety. Guests spread warm cheese on slices of homemade whole-wheat bread.

Cheese Wrapped in Pastry

Beet and Radish Salad

Glühwein
GLOW WINE

FAR LEFT: *We set this afternoon feast on a woven Christmas throw on top of a low coffee table, then moved it in front of the fireplace, where Ruth and friends gathered to finish needlepoint presents.*

◈45◈

Cheese Wrapped in Pastry

I. Camembert in Phyllo Weave

6 sheets frozen phyllo dough, about 12¾ x9 inches each, thawed
1 tablespoon unsalted butter, melted
3 4-ounce rounds Camembert cheese

Preheat oven to 350° F. Lightly grease a baking sheet and set aside.

Carefully lay out 1 sheet of phyllo on a cutting board and fold into quarters. Brush lightly with butter. Place 1 cheese round in the center of phyllo and wrap the dough around the cheese, molding the corners over the top.

From the wide end of another sheet of dough, cut six ½-inch strips. Working quickly, weave strips to form a lattice on top of cheese, tucking ends under. Repeat the process with remaining 2 cheeses. Place on baking sheet and set aside while you make the following varieties.

II. Camembert in an Open Phyllo Shell

9 sheets frozen phyllo dough, about 12¾ x9 inches each, thawed
1 tablespoon unsalted butter, melted
3 4-ounce rounds pepper-crust or plain Camembert cheese
6 sun-dried tomato slices, soaked in water overnight and drained

Prepare the dough, folding in quarters and brushing lightly with butter, as in variation I. Place 1 cheese round in the center of dough and wrap dough around the cheese to cover the sides only, molding and tucking to leave the top surface uncovered. Lightly butter another sheet of dough. Fold it lengthwise in 1-inch increments, accor-

dion-style. Then loosely twist the folded strip of dough a few times to form a thin rope. Wrap twisted phyllo rope tightly around circumference of cheese, starting at the very bottom. Repeat with another sheet of phyllo and continue wrapping up the outside of the cheese until rope comes to the rim. If the cheese is plain, without the pepper crust, cut top rind off the cheese with a small sharp knife. Decorate with 2 tomato slices. Repeat with remaining 2 cheeses and place on prepared baking sheet with the lattice-top cheeses. Set aside while you make the following varieties.

III. Camembert in Phyllo with a Bow

6 sheets frozen phyllo dough, about 12¾ x9 inches each, thawed
1 tablespoon unsalted butter, melted
3 sun-dried tomato slices, soaked in water overnight and drained
9 green peppercorns packed in brine, drained
3 4-ounce rounds Camembert cheese

Prepare 3 sheets of dough, folding into quarters and brushing lightly with butter, as in variation I. Place 1 tomato slice and 3 peppercorns on top of 1 cheese round. Lay the dough over the top of cheese and wrap it around the sides, pinching to seal on the bottom of cheese.

Cut another sheet of dough lengthwise into 9 1-inch strips. Fold each in half lengthwise to form ½-inch strips. Working quickly, lay 2 strips on top of cheese, crisscrossing in the center and tucking ends under. Use a third strip to form a bow, then place it on top of the 2 strips and pinch them all together in the center. Smooth the ends of the bow down the side of the cheese, tucking the ends under. Repeat process with remaining 2 cheeses and place on prepared baking sheet with the other varieties. Set aside while you make recipe below.

IV. CAMEMBERT IN A PHYLLO POUCH

3 sheets frozen phyllo dough, about 12¾ x 9 inches each,
  thawed
1 tablespoon unsalted butter, melted
3 4-ounce rounds Camembert cheese

Prepare the dough, folding into quarters and brushing lightly with butter, as in variation I. Place 1 cheese in center of the dough and wrap dough around the sides and up the top, pinching corners together to create a topknot. Repeat with remaining 2 cheeses and place on the baking sheet with the other 3 varieties.

Bake all varieties together until golden, about 15 minutes. Let stand a few minutes before serving.

૭ૅ ૨ય

ABOVE: *From Flat Earth Clay Works, we collect Santa ceramics in red and green. These plates, as well as the matching mugs, make wonderful gifts when the plates are filled with cookies and the mugs are stuffed full of cinnamon sticks. A bow made of sun-dried tomatoes adorns the baked cheese.*

BEET AND RADISH SALAD

The delicious character of this salad comes from the contrast between the tender beets and the crisp radish. If you have any left over, refrigerate it overnight and puree it the next day. Serve it warm or as a cold soup, topped with a dollop of yogurt or sour cream. If you end up with red fingers after peeling the fresh beets, use fresh lemon juice to clean your hands.

2 bunches fresh beets (about 10–12 large), or 2 16-ounce cans medium-sized cooked beets, drained
1 teaspoon salt
1 teaspoon cider vinegar
12 medium red radishes, trimmed, washed, and sliced
2 tablespoons balsamic vinegar
¼ teaspoon freshly ground pepper
¼ teaspoon caraway seeds
2 tablespoons olive oil
6 large leaves red leaf lettuce

Wash and trim the fresh beets, leaving about 1 inch of stem. Place in a saucepan. Add just enough water to cover, ½ teaspoon of the salt, and the cider vinegar. Heat to boiling, reduce heat, and simmer, covered, until beets are tender, about 30 minutes. Drain and rinse in ice-cold water. Set 1 beet aside for garnish. Holding each beet by the stem, peel and slice into ⅛-inch-thick slices.

If you're using canned beets, cut each in half and do not save one for garnish (since it has no stem).

Place the fresh or canned beets and the radishes in a serving bowl. Combine the balsamic vinegar, the remaining ½ teaspoon salt, the pepper, and the caraway seeds in a small bowl. Whisk in the oil. Pour over beets and toss to coat well. Let stand at least 30 minutes at room temperature. To serve, place the reserved whole fresh beet on top of the salad in the bowl. Place a large leaf of red leaf lettuce on each of the 6 plates and spoon the salad onto the leaves.

Glühwein
Glow Wine

1 750-ml. bottle red wine
5 whole cloves
2 cinnamon sticks
¼ cup sugar
Juice of ½ lemon
Zest of ½ lemon
¼ cup dark rum (optional)
6 cinnamon sticks for garnish

Combine all ingredients in a medium saucepan. Heat to simmering; do not boil. Strain if you want to (we don't) and keep warm. To serve, ladle into mugs and add a cinnamon stick to each mug. *Serves 6.*

ABOVE: *The red of these beets contrasts with the green of the throw to create a visual feast.*

A Bakery at Home

For true fresh bread lovers, the bread machine is a great addition to today's kitchen. Not only does it make loaves of fresh whole-wheat, seven-grain, cranberry, and Irish soda breads, it also produces rolls and pastries. Programming it ahead, we made two beautiful loaves for our Saint Nicholas Day party. The machine will bake the bread overnight, waking you up with a delicious aroma. What a simple way to bake your Christmas gift breads too! Frozen fresh, they keep perfectly for weeks. In addition to making bread, some machines can even prepare fresh jams and steam rice.

We have also discovered from friends and husbands of friends that the machine is a perfect present for the gadget-loving gourmet man in the family.

Good-looking and good-tasting country breads are also available in bakeries and in some supermarkets. There are also fine bakeries all over the country that ship mail orders. For years we have ordered the large loaves of Holzofen Brot from Canada for our big parties.

Recently, we've discovered wonderful brick-oven breads closer to home at Dan Leader's Bread Alone Bakery in Boiceville, New York. He will also ship overnight and his breads are well worth the effort of the phone call.

ABOVE: *A basket full of home-baked bread, herbed vinegar and oil, apples, cheese, and cinnamon star cookies awaits Saint Nicholas when he comes during the night to pick up the wish lists.* LEFT: *Loaves of peasant bread, wheat-walnut, sourdough, and mixed-grain bread from Bread Alone Bakery warm on the stove, creating a perfume through the house that smells as if we were baking the bread ourselves.*

Second Week of Advent

COUNTRY POT PIE DINNER FOR TEN

⚜

W e light two candles now on our Advent wreath and sit down to an early dinner of country pot pies for family, neighbors, and close friends—Hans and Sandra, Keiran and Kythera, Fay and Bud, Lans and Debbe. The pies will stay warm through second helpings while we take plenty of time to talk, reminisce, and plan the coming weeks.

We are all deeper into Christmas preparations, and the excitement is beginning to grow. *Winter Holiday*, the album of Christmas music, is playing in the background. Skitch remembers the rehearsals and recording it with the New York Philharmonic in 1962. It has become a standard at our house.

Keiran and Kythera are rehearsing each day at school for the Christmas concert and are already experiencing pre-performance jitters. They are also preparing for winter solstice—a big event at the Montessori school. Keiran tells us that it's a celebration of light. Kythera adds that it's a time to nurture your inner self, bringing light within while the darkness grows outside.

There is a call from Germany!—just as we have served up the last helping and steam is rising from our plates. We're not surprised. Each year there is a long-distance telephone reunion for Ruth and her best pals from kindergarten—Käte, Dieter, and Ilse. Ruth arranges a time to call them back and returns to dinner, but the call has sparked memories that come pouring out. Like Keiran and Kythera, Ruth performed at school in the Christmas pageant. Every child got a part no matter what. Ruth was a *Hirte*, or shepherd, who

Turkey Pot Pie for Ten

*Ruth's Easy
Cranberry Walnut Crunch*

Beef Pot Pie for Ten

*Lans's Best
Horseradish*

Vegetable Pot Pie

Brioche Crust

*Orange Apricot Raspberry
Trifle*

◆51◆

FAR LEFT: *At this dinner, one of us sits at each end of the long table and serves our guests from the big pies. For seconds, everybody helps himself. We brought out our best crystal to contrast with the rustic pottery.*

ABOVE: *Before the meal, the whole room is lit by candles. There's a spinning pyramid ornament in place of the pot pies and our handcrafted Mexican goblets are filled with votive lights.*

RIGHT: *At the base of the candle-powered pyramid is a hand-carved Nativity scene.*

got to tend real live lambs and sheep on stage. They were the true stars of the show. There was a real donkey in the stable too. And Ruth, in spite of paralyzing stage fright, got to speak her first lines: *"Der Stern! Der Stern!"* ("The star"), she shouted, with one arm pointing to the suspended golden star above the stable.

After the pageant came *Weihnachtsferien*—Christmas vacation. At home for the next weeks, Ruth would find her days full of activities. She and her best pals would get to bake with Liesel, the family cook. There would be dozens of Christmas breads and hundreds of cookies. Liesel was magic with little children, giving each a bowl of cookie dough and a pastry bag full of frosting to decorate the cookies when they cooled. Sometimes dough ended up on elbows, knees, and floor, but Liesel showed endless patience and good nature.

There would be other projects during the day too, like embroidering pillow covers and spreads and whittling wood for gifts. And right after dinner each night came the best treat of all, *rodeln* (sleigh riding) in the center of town. The hilly snow-covered streets were closed to traffic and the children rode their sleds under the light of streetlamps. Then, before bed, the radio played the songs of Christmas. Men with soothing voices read poems and troupes of actors

read Christmas plays—always a story of an unexpected homecoming, or of a child rewarded for good deeds, or of a nonbeliever who by some miracle gets the Christmas spirit.

The memories and stories around the table now are as flavorful as the steaming pies. The easy, leisurely meal belies the bustle of projects to come in the week ahead. But the pot pies, full of meat, potatoes, and vegetables and topped with a golden brioche crust so thick it becomes the bread of the meal, are made hearty for rich, long-lasting sustenance. We bake turkey, beef, and vegetable pot pies. Leftover pies are frozen and used weeks later. Delicious!

LEFT: *Our Advent wreath is skirted with fresh greens. A small clay pot with a topiary inside is the place-card holder.*

❖ 53 ❖

TURKEY POT PIE FOR TEN

This pie has a hearty look—the pieces of turkey are large and the vegetables are larger than bite-size. It looks like a whole meal on the plate, with ample portions of turkey, vegetables, potatoes, and gravy.

To get our turkey slices, we roasted a 21-pound turkey the day before and left on the golden-brown skin.

ABOVE: *We roasted a whole turkey for our pot pie, but a roasted turkey breast would also do just fine. The whole turkey will yield enough meat for two more meals. The triple steamer holds all the vegetables for all the pies.*

1 lemon, sliced
1 sprig fresh marjoram or 1 teaspoon dried marjoram
3 pounds sweet potatoes (about 6 medium), peeled and cut in half lengthwise
2 pounds fresh Brussels sprouts, washed and trimmed
10 medium carrots, peeled
12 small white onions, peeled
15 mushrooms, wiped clean and cut in half
4 pounds white turkey meat with skin, cut in ¼-to-½-inch-thick slices

GRAVY
½ cup (1 stick) unsalted butter
1½ cups flour
1 tablespoon salt
1 tablespoon freshly ground pepper
2 teaspoons dried marjoram
4 quarts warm turkey stock or warm canned chicken broth

Brioche Crust (see recipe, page 61)
1 large egg
1 tablespoon milk
Ruth's Easy Cranberry Walnut Crunch (see recipe, page 55)

Fill the bottom of a large vegetable steamer with water. Add the lemon and marjoram to the water. Place the potatoes in the steamer basket and fit into the pot (make sure water does not touch basket). Heat to boiling, cover, and steam until just tender, about 8 to 10 minutes. Transfer the potatoes to a bowl or plate. Add the Brussels sprouts to the steamer basket; cover and steam until just tender, about 5 minutes. Transfer the sprouts to a bowl or plate. Add the carrots and onions to the steamer basket; cover and steam 5 minutes.

Preheat oven to 400° F.

Arrange the steamed vegetables, mushrooms, and turkey in an attractive 5–6-quart (ours was 9x12x3 inches) ovenproof casserole and set aside.

To make the gravy, melt butter in a large saucepan over medium heat. Whisk in the flour. Cook, whisking constantly, until golden brown.

Whisk in the salt, pepper, marjoram, and warm stock. Reduce heat and simmer, stirring gently, until gravy thickens, about 8 minutes.

Fill the casserole with enough gravy to come within ½ inch of the top. Save excess gravy for another time.

Roll the brioche dough into a ¼-inch-thick circle large enough to cover the casserole. Fit the dough over the casserole, then trim, flute, and pinch the edges to seal the casserole rim. Reserve excess dough. Beat the egg and the milk in a small bowl. Cut 4 vents in the brioche top and brush the top lightly with the egg mixture.

Bake until the crust is brown, about 1½ hours. Cover lightly with foil or parchment if top browns too quickly.

Meanwhile, roll out the reserved brioche dough to ⅛-inch thickness. Using 2¼- or 3-inch animal-shaped cookie cutters, cut out as many shapes as possible. Place the shaped dough on a lightly greased cookie sheet, brush lightly with egg mixture, and bake on a separate rack in the same oven until puffed and golden, about 25 minutes. To serve, place the animal shapes as decorations on the finished pie. Pass Ruth's Easy Cranberry Walnut Crunch on the side. *Serves 10.*

☙ ❧

ABOVE LEFT AND RIGHT: *All our pot pies use the same kinds of vegetables, except that the turkey pie calls for sweet potatoes and the beef pie calls for red potatoes. The cow and chicken pastry cutouts identify the pies. We baked them separately and placed them on top of the baked pies.*

RUTH'S EASY CRANBERRY WALNUT CRUNCH

Here is another condiment that makes a fine gift for the pantry. This recipe makes more than you will need for the meal. Spoon the extra amount into a sterilized jar. Seal, process in a hot-water bath, and store in a cool place until gift-giving time!

4 cups fresh cranberries, washed and picked over
1 cup light brown sugar, firmly packed
½ teaspoon ground cloves
1 cup walnuts, coarsely chopped

Combine the cranberries, sugar, and cloves in a medium saucepan. Heat over medium heat, stirring constantly but very gently, until sugar is dissolved. Try to keep the cranberries whole. Gently fold in the walnuts and cook, stirring gently, over low heat for an additional 5 minutes. Serve warm or cold. *Makes 5–6 cups.*

☙ ❧

TURKEY POT PIE FOR TWO

1 lemon, sliced

1 sprig fresh marjoram or 1 teaspoon dried marjoram

1 large sweet potato, peeled and cut into 2-inch pieces

6 fresh Brussels sprouts, washed and trimmed

1 large carrot, peeled and cut into 2-inch pieces

2 small white onions, peeled

2 mushrooms, wiped clean and cut in half

¾ pound white turkey meat, cut in 1- and 2-inch pieces

GRAVY

¼ cup (4 tablespoons) unsalted butter

¾–1 cup flour

1 teaspoon salt

1 teaspoon freshly ground pepper

1 teaspoon dried marjoram

1½ quarts warm turkey stock or warm canned chicken broth

Half recipe Brioche Crust (see recipe, page 61)

1 large egg

1 tablespoon milk

Follow directions for Turkey Pot Pie for Ten recipe on page 54. Put ingredients into a 1-quart ovenproof casserole and bake until crust is brown, about 45 minutes.

෨ ෨

ABOVE RIGHT: *To serve this beef pot pie for two steaming hot, we use Robert Parrott's oval platter as an underplate.*

BEEF POT PIE FOR TEN

MARINADE

½ cup lemon juice

1 tablespoon green peppercorns packed in brine, drained

2 bay leaves

1 tablespoon olive oil

4 pounds flank steak (2 fillets, each about 2 inches thick)

1–2 bottles (750 ml. each) red wine

2 tablespoons unsalted butter

GRAVY

4 ounces dried wild mushrooms

½ cup (1 stick) unsalted butter

1½ cups flour

1 tablespoon salt

1 tablespoon freshly ground pepper

2 teaspoons dried marjoram

3 quarts warm beef stock or warm canned beef broth

1 lemon, sliced

1 sprig fresh marjoram or 1 teaspoon dried marjoram

18 small red potatoes

1½ pounds fresh Brussels sprouts, washed and trimmed

10 medium carrots, peeled

12 small white onions, peeled

2½ cups diced celery (about 6 stalks)

15 mushrooms, wiped clean and cut in half

Brioche Crust (see recipe, page 61)

1 large egg

1 tablespoon milk

Lans's Best Horseradish (recipe follows)

To make the marinade, combine the lemon juice, peppercorns, bay leaves, and olive oil in a small bowl. Mix well.

Place the meat in a deep ceramic dish and rub with marinade. Add enough red wine to cover. Cover with plastic wrap and refrigerate overnight. Remove meat from marinade and pat dry. Strain marinade and reserve.

Heat the 2 tablespoons butter in a large skillet over medium-high heat. Add the meat and sear until very brown but not burned, about 5 minutes per side. Reduce heat and cook 5 minutes longer. (If you want your meat to be falling-apart tender, cook 10 minutes longer.) Transfer meat to a cutting board and reserve pan juices. Allow meat to cool slightly, then slice in ⅛-inch-thick slices.

To make the gravy, place the dried mushrooms in a small bowl and cover with 1 cup warm water. Let stand at least 20 minutes. Meanwhile, melt the ½ cup butter in a large saucepan over medium-high heat. Whisk in the flour and cook, whisking constantly, until flour is a rich, dark brown. Whisk in the salt, pepper, marjoram, beef stock, and re-

served marinade. Reduce heat and cook, stirring gently but constantly, until mixture thickens, about 8 minutes. Add mushrooms and reserved pan juices. Keep warm.

Preheat the oven to 400° F.

Fill the bottom of a large vegetable steamer with water. Add lemon and marjoram to water. Place potatoes in the steamer basket and fit into the pot (make sure water does not touch basket). Heat to boiling, cover, and steam until barely tender, about 7 minutes. Transfer to a plate or bowl. Add the Brussels sprouts to the steamer basket; cover and continue steaming 7 minutes. Transfer to a bowl or plate. Add the carrots and onions to steamer basket; cover and steam 5 minutes.

Arrange the steamed vegetables, celery, mushrooms, and beef in a 5–6-quart 9x12x3-inch oven-proof casserole. Fill with enough gravy to come within ½ inch of the top. Save excess gravy for another time.

Roll the brioche dough into a ¼-inch-thick circle large enough to cover the casserole. Fit the dough over the casserole, then trim, flute, and pinch the edges to seal to rim. Reserve excess dough. Beat the egg and the milk in a small bowl. Cut 4 vents in brioche top and brush lightly with egg mixture.

Bake until crust is golden brown, about 1½ hours. Cover lightly with foil or parchment if top browns too quickly.

Meanwhile, roll out the reserved brioche dough to ⅛-inch thickness. Using 2¼- or 3-inch animal cookie cutters, cut out as many shapes as possible. Place on a lightly greased cookie sheet and bake on a separate rack in the same oven until puffed and golden, about 25 minutes. To serve, place animal shapes as decorations on the finished pie. Pass Lans's Best Horseradish on the side. *Serves 10.*

LANS'S BEST HORSERADISH

Lans Christensen is not only a gifted photographer, he's an inventive and generous cook besides. We loved his best horseradish!

14 ounces ketchup
12 ounces fresh horseradish, peeled and grated
1 tablespoon prepared mustard

Combine all ingredients in the container of a food processor fitted with the metal blade. Process until roughly combined. Serve with Beef Pot Pie. Keeps in a sealed jar in the refrigerator up to 6 weeks. *Makes about 3 cups.*

୧୭ ୨୭

BEEF POT PIE FOR TWO

MARINADE

¼ cup lemon juice
1 teaspoon green peppercorns packed in brine, drained
1 bay leaf
1 teaspoon olive oil
1 2-inch-thick flank steak (about ¾ pound), cut into
    cubes
2 cups red wine

1 tablespoon unsalted butter

GRAVY

1 ounce dried wild mushrooms
4 tablespoons (½ stick) unsalted butter
1 cup flour

1 teaspoon salt
1 teaspoon freshly ground pepper
1 teaspoon dried marjoram
1 quart warm beef stock or warm canned beef broth

1 lemon, sliced
1 sprig fresh marjoram or 1 teaspoon dried marjoram
3 small red potatoes
6 fresh Brussels sprouts, washed and trimmed
1 large carrot, peeled and cut into 2-inch pieces
2 small white onions, peeled
½ cup diced celery (about 1 stalk)
2 mushrooms, wiped clean and cut in half

Half recipe Brioche Crust (see recipe, page 61)
1 large egg
1 tablespoon milk

Follow directions for Beef Pot Pie for Ten recipe on page 56.

Put ingredients into a 1-quart ovenproof casserole and bake until crust is brown, about 45 minutes.

❧ ❧

❖ 59 ❖

ABOVE LEFT: *Carved from a single branch, a rooster by Kentucky artist Minnie Adkins joins a dinner for two. There's really enough for four, but we've never been afraid of leftovers.*

RIGHT: *At our sit-down dinner for ten, Skitch was in charge of serving the hearty Beef Pot Pie.*

VEGETABLE POT PIE

We have vegetarian friends who aren't afraid to come to our house for dinner. There's always something hearty for them to eat.

1 lemon, quartered
2 sprigs fresh or dried marjoram, or ½ teaspoon dried marjoram
6 small red potatoes
12 fresh Brussels sprouts, washed and trimmed
3 medium carrots, peeled
6 small white onions, peeled
1 whole leek, white part only, washed well
4 mushrooms, wiped clean and cut in half

GRAVY
2 tablespoons unsalted butter
½ cup flour
3 cups milk, scalded
¼ teaspoon white pepper
Salt to taste
1 cup warm vegetable stock

Brioche Crust (see recipe, page 61)
1 large egg
1 tablespoon milk

Preheat the oven to 400° F.

Fill the bottom of a large vegetable steamer with water. Add the lemon and marjoram to water. Place the potatoes and Brussels sprouts in the steamer basket and fit into the steamer (make sure water does not touch basket). Heat to boiling, cover, and steam 2 minutes. Add the carrots, onions, and leek; cover and continue steaming 5 minutes. Place the steamed vegetables and mushrooms in an ovenproof 1½-quart casserole and set aside.

To make the gravy, melt the butter in the top portion of a double boiler over simmering water. Whisk in the flour. Gradually add the milk, whisking constantly until mixture thickens. Add the pepper and salt to taste. Whisk in the broth. Stir until mixture is thick, about 3 minutes. Pour enough gravy into the casserole to cover vegetables and reserve excess for another time.

Roll brioche dough into a ¼-inch-thick circle large enough to cover the casserole. Fit the dough over the casserole, then trim, flute, and pinch the edges to seal to rim. Beat the egg and the milk in a small bowl. Cut 4 vents in brioche top and brush lightly with the egg mixture.

Bake until crust is golden brown, about 45 minutes. *Serves 2–4.*

৯৯ ৶

ABOVE: *On some occasions, we bake and serve our Vegetable Pot Pie in horseshoe-shaped pottery from Cornelius Rotter of Austria.*

BRIOCHE CRUST

A thick and rich addition to our pot pies, this top crust is more a bread than a pastry. We like the extra richness with our winter meals.

2 tablespoons sugar
½ cup warm water
1 package (¼ ounce) active dry yeast
1 cup (2 sticks) butter, softened
6 large eggs at room temperature, lightly beaten
1 tablespoon salt
4–5 cups sifted flour

Dissolve the sugar in the water in a small bowl. Sprinkle in the yeast and stir; let stand until bubbles form, about 3 minutes. Transfer to the bowl of an electric mixer. Add butter, eggs, salt, and 3 cups of the flour. Beat at medium speed for 4 minutes, scraping the sides with a spatula. Continue beating on low speed and add enough of the remaining flour to make the dough smooth and elastic.

Shape dough into a ball and place in a lightly oiled ceramic bowl. Cover with a clean damp towel and place in a warm, draft-free place until doubled in size, about 1½ hours. Punch down the dough, cover, and place in refrigerator for 8 hours. Watch dough carefully: if it rises above rim while in the refrigerator, gently punch it down. Keep refrigerated until ready to use. *Makes enough to top 1 large casserole.*

❧ ❧

ORANGE APRICOT RASPBERRY TRIFLE

This is a showy dessert, perfect for a festive supper. It's probably the fanciest thing we do during the Christmas season.

CAKE
6 large eggs at room temperature, separated
2 cups cake flour (not self-rising)
1 cup water
1 tablespoon baking powder
½ teaspoon orange-flower water or ¼ teaspoon orange extract
¼ teaspoon salt
½ cup sugar
½ teaspoon cream of tartar

ORANGE CREAM
12 egg yolks
1⅓ cups sugar
3 cups hot milk
2 tablespoons vanilla extract
6 tablespoons (¾ stick) unsalted butter, cut into bits
1 tablespoon orange zest

FILLING
12 ounces dried apricots, quartered
2½ cups Marsala
2 cups heavy cream
1 tablespoon confectioners' sugar
1 teaspoon vanilla extract
8 ounces raspberry jam
6 ounces blanched slivered almonds, toasted
3 tablespoons bittersweet chocolate shavings for garnish

To make the cake, preheat the oven to 350° F. Line two 8-inch round cake pans with parchment paper. Lightly grease and flour the parchment.

Combine the egg yolks, flour, water, baking powder, orange-flower water, salt, and ¼ cup of the sugar in a large bowl. Beat until light, about 3 minutes.

In another bowl, beat the egg whites and cream of tartar, adding remaining ¼ cup sugar 2 tablespoons at a time until whites are stiff but not dry.

Gently fold the whites into the flour mixture just until blended. Pour evenly into the prepared pans. Bake until the top of the cake springs back when lightly pressed with fingertips, about 25 minutes. Cool the cakes in the pans on a wire rack. Unmold when completely cooled.

To make the Orange Cream, combine the egg yolks and sugar in a medium saucepan; whisk until thick and light in color. Gradually add the hot milk and stir with a wooden spoon. Heat over medium heat, stirring constantly, until mixture coats the back of the spoon. DO NOT BOIL. Remove from heat, then stir in the vanilla, butter, and orange zest. Chill at least 2 hours.

Meanwhile, make the filling. Place the apricots in a medium bowl. Add the Marsala and let stand until plumped, about 1 hour. Drain and reserve the Marsala.

Beat the cream with the confectioners' sugar and vanilla in a large bowl until stiff peaks form. Set aside.

To assemble the trifle, cut each cake in half horizontally using a serrated knife. Place one cake layer in the bottom of an 8-inch, 3-quart trifle bowl. Brush with ¼ of the reserved Marsala and cover with ¼ of the jam. Sprinkle with ¼ of the apricots and spread with ¼ of the orange cream. Sprinkle on 2 tablespoons of the almonds. Repeat this process with the remaining 3 cake layers, pressing gently after adding each cake layer. Top with whipped cream and sprinkle with any remaining almonds and the chocolate shavings. *Serves 10.*

RIGHT: *Since the trifle is a rich dessert, we serve small helpings from the sideboard. Nobody notices who takes seconds!*

ANGEL FOOD DESSERT BUFFET

This is a perfect late-night or afternoon party, especially after caroling. Baking for this dessert buffet is usually our first cookie project of the season and reminds Ruth of her childhood in Germany, when she would try to snitch a finger full of dough in her mother's kitchen. "Don't eat unbaked dough," her mother always warned. "Your stomach will stick together."

We still make enough dough for several snitched fingerfuls! And we bake enough cookies so that we can pack some away in tins for Christmas gifts or for easy desserts in the coming weeks.

*Heavenly Lemon
Raspberry Hearts*

Cinnamon Stars

Star Light Meringues

*Angel Cake with
Lemon Glaze*

Holiday Punch

❖65❖

FAR LEFT: *Angels made by Mary Ann Sabados grace our dessert buffet.*

Equipment for All Cookie Projects

COOKIE CUTTERS ◆ DISPOSABLE PASTRY BAGS ◆ PARCHMENT PAPER ◆
ROLLING PIN ◆ 2 COOKIE SHEETS, OR 4 IF POSSIBLE ◆
TINS AND GIFT CONTAINERS

Start a collection of different shapes and sizes of cookie cutters—as many as you can. There are even mini-cutters available for tiny cookies. Cookie cutters also make delightful gifts. Tie a bow on one and give it as an ornament. If you can't find the perfect shape for the perfect cookie, draw a template of your own on heavy cardboard and cut it out. Use the template instead of a cookie cutter, placing it on rolled-out cookie dough and cut around the edge with a sharp knife. Start collecting tins early and continue all year round. They must be airtight. Line them with colored foils to guarantee freshness and add a festive look.

THE ANGEL DECORATION

Her poise is the result of old-fashioned fabric starch. Once shaped, she keeps watch over your Christmas season from year to year. Allow 2 days to complete this project and by all means include the children. All the materials can be found at craft stores, hobby stores, florists, and hardware and grocery stores.

Aluminum foil
Plastic wrap
Styrofoam cone or empty bottle (see below for sizes)
Styrofoam ball (see below)
Straight pins and toothpicks
Cheesecloth 36 inches wide, sold by the yard (see below for sizes)
Liquid fabric starch
Gallon-size zip-close plastic bags
Thread
Spanish moss
Glue gun
Star garland (foil stars on flexible wire)
Paper Twist (paper ribbon sold by the yard; see below for quantity)

1. To begin, choose what size angel or angels you want to make. This list will allow you to gather materials for one angel or a family of angels of different sizes.

15-INCH ANGEL
3-liter soda bottle for the body
5-inch Styrofoam ball for the head
Cheesecloth circle for dress, 36 inches in diameter
Cheesecloth rectangle for sleeves, 10x15 inches
Paper Twist for wings, 9x30 inches

12-INCH ANGEL
1-liter soda bottle for the body
3½-inch Styrofoam ball for the head
Cheesecloth circle for dress, 30 inches in diameter

Cheesecloth rectangle for sleeves, 9x14 inches
Paper Twist for wings, 7½x26 inches

10-INCH ANGEL
Ketchup or beer bottle for the body
3-inch Styrofoam ball for the head
Cheesecloth circle for dress, 23 inches in diameter
Cheesecloth rectangle for sleeves, 6x11 inches
Paper Twist for wings, 6x22 inches

5-INCH ANGEL
Vanilla extract bottle for the body
1-inch Styrofoam ball for the head
Cheesecloth circle for dress, 12 inches in diameter
Cheesecloth rectangle for sleeves, 4x6 inches
Paper Twist for wings, 3x12 inches

2. When you have gathered your equipment and supplies, cover your work area with aluminum foil.

3. Cover the cone or bottle base with plastic wrap, leaving neck edge uncovered if using a bottle. Attach angel head (ball) to top of cone using toothpicks or to top of bottle neck by pushing ball down on neck of bottle.

4. Cut cheesecloth into desired-sized circle. Pour 1 to 1½ cups liquid starch into a zip-close plastic bag. Thoroughly soak fabric in the starch. Remove and squeeze out excess. Center fabric over the head and smooth down so that the head is completely covered. Arrange the folds around the body and the base to create an angel's robe.

5. Cut a thread 12 to 15 inches in length and tie it around the base of the ball to form the fabric into a neck. Let dry overnight on the work surface. Remove the thread.

6. Cut a rectangular piece of cheesecloth into the desired size for the sleeves. Pour 1 to 1½ cups liquid starch into a zip-close plastic bag. Soak fabric as you did in step 4, squeezing out excess as before. Fold in half lengthwise and drape over figure,

centering fabric in angel's shoulder area. Shape as you like. You may need to pin sleeves to the base at the shoulders while fabric is drying.

7. Shape Spanish moss into a ball and, using a glue gun, glue "hair" to top of head.

8. Make a halo from the star garland by forming one long length of garland into a stem with a circle on top. Strip the stars from the stem of the halo. Glue halo stem to the angel's back.

9. Cut a rectangle of Paper Twist into the desired size. Fold the short edges of the ribbon over each other so that they extend 1 inch beyond midpoint. Pinch the ribbon at midpoint and tie with a 1-inch-wide strip of ribbon. These are the wings. Glue them to the back of the angel with the knotted side facing in.

10. Let angel dry on work surface. You may remove the cone or bottle from the angel when dry if desired.

ཥ ཤ

ABOVE: *The secret to an eye-catching buffet is to create surprise by serving from a variety of levels and adding contrasting textures. Here, cake stands provide height. An evergreen wreath decorated with hydrangeas and bunches of dried brownii, an Australian plant, is one of our favorite touches.*

HEAVENLY LEMON RASPBERRY HEARTS

We made 2 different-sized hearts, sometimes placing the smaller on top of the larger. Experiment to treat your own eye.

1 ¾ cups flour
3 tablespoons cornstarch
½ teaspoon baking powder
Pinch of salt
½ cup (1 stick) butter, softened
¼ cup sugar
1 egg, lightly beaten
1 teaspoon lemon extract
Raspberry Frost (recipe follows)

Preheat oven to 375° F. Lightly grease 2 cookie sheets and set aside.

Combine the flour, cornstarch, baking powder, and salt in a medium bowl. Set aside.

Beat the butter and sugar in a large bowl until creamy and light. Add the egg, then the lemon extract, beating well after each addition. Gradually sift in the flour mixture and continue beating until dough cleans the sides of the bowl and forms a ball.

Roll the dough out on a lightly floured board to ⅛-inch thickness. Using a 2½-inch and a 2-inch heart-shaped cookie cutter, cut cookies from the dough and place on the prepared cookie sheets. Bake until lightly golden, about 15 minutes. Cool completely on a rack. Decorate with Raspberry Frost. Let dry completely, then store in airtight containers until Christmas. *Makes about 2½–3 dozen, depending on the size of the cookie cutter.*

RASPBERRY FROST

1 12-ounce package frozen raspberries
3 tablespoons water
2 cups confectioners' sugar

Heat the raspberries and the water in a saucepan over medium heat until completely thawed. Place in the container of a blender and blend until smooth. Strain through a fine sieve.

Combine the sugar and strained raspberry juice in a medium bowl; beat until smooth. *Makes 2 cups.*

ABOVE: *On this handmade Advent calendar, each number is actually a pocket containing a tiny ornament for the tree. As the days pass, the tree is covered with more and more decorations.*

RIGHT: *Stars and hearts and meringues—these are our favorites for giving away. Have cellophane bags and ribbon ready and let your guests package their own for a take-home gift.*

CINNAMON STARS

We used different-sized star-shaped cutters for these cookies—2¼-inch, 3-inch, and 4-inch. Some we frosted, some we left plain. You can create a variety as well.

5½ cups flour
3 teaspoons cinnamon
¾ teaspoon salt
1½ cups sugar
1 cup (2 sticks) unsalted butter, softened
2 large eggs, lightly beaten
½ cup dark molasses
3 teaspoons baking soda
2 cups confectioners' sugar

Preheat the oven to 375° F. Lightly grease 2 cookie sheets and set aside.

Combine the flour, cinnamon, and salt in a large bowl. Set aside.

Beat the sugar and the butter in a large bowl until creamy and light. Add the eggs, then the molasses, beating well after each addition. Dissolve the baking soda in ½ cup water and beat into the batter. Gradually add the flour mixture and stir until well combined and a soft dough forms. Shape into a ball and return to bowl; then cover with plastic wrap and refrigerate at least 2 hours.

Roll the dough out on a lightly floured surface to ⅛-inch thickness. Using a variety of star-shaped cookie cutters, cut the dough into shapes. Place about 2 inches apart on cookie sheets. Bake until lightly golden, about 10 minutes. Cool completely on a rack.

For the frosting, combine the confectioners' sugar and ¼ cup water in a medium bowl. Holding the stars by the edges, dip each one in the frosting so that the top surface is completely coated. Let dry completely before storing in airtight containers.
Makes 5 to 6 dozen, depending on the size of cookie cutters.

STAR LIGHT MERINGUES

3 egg whites
½ teaspoon cream of tartar
¼ teaspoon salt
1 teaspoon almond extract
¾ cup sugar

Preheat the oven to 300° F. Line two 15x18-inch cookie sheets with parchment paper and place another cookie sheet under each lined sheet. Set aside.

Beat the egg whites, cream of tartar, salt, and almond extract in the bowl of an electric mixer until soft peaks form. Gradually add ½ the sugar, beating it in 2 tablespoons at a time until whites are stiff but not dry. Fold in remaining sugar. Spoon batter into a pastry bag fitted with a star tip and pipe stars 1 inch apart onto prepared cookie sheets.

Bake for 20 minutes, then turn the oven off. Open the oven door and leave it ajar for 30 minutes. Gently peel stars off the parchment and cool completely on a rack. Store in airtight containers.
Makes 4 dozen.

ANGEL CAKE WITH LEMON GLAZE

A light and delightful dessert, this is always one of our favorites. Try decorating with the Star Light Meringues, as we did, or serve it plain. We have also frozen this cake for up to one month. The results . . . delicious.

CAKE

1 cup sifted cake flour (not self-rising)

1½ cups superfine sugar

12 egg whites

1½ teaspoons cream of tartar

1½ teaspoons vanilla extract

¼ teaspoon salt

GLAZE

4 cups confectioners' sugar, sifted

1 cup milk

2 tablespoons lemon juice

To make the cake, preheat the oven to 375° F.

Sift the flour and ¾ cup of the sugar together in a large bowl. Sift again and set aside.

Beat the egg whites, cream of tartar, vanilla, and salt together in a large bowl until soft peaks form. Add the remaining ¾ cup sugar 2 table-spoons at a time, and continue beating until the whites are stiff but not dry. Sift in ¼ of the flour mixture and gently fold to blend. Fold in remaining flour, adding ¼ of the mixture at a time. Turn the batter into an ungreased 10-inch tube pan. Bake until lightly golden and a toothpick inserted in the center comes out clean, about 35 minutes. Invert cake pan over a bottle until completely cool, about 1½ hours. Loosen edges with a sharp knife and unmold onto a cake plate.

For the glaze, combine the sugar and milk in a small saucepan. Cook over low heat until sugar is completely dissolved. Cool. Stir in the lemon juice and drizzle over top of cake. *Serves 12.*

❧ ❧

LEFT: A lime makes a perfect clove holder, providing color and flavor while keeping the cloves out of individual servings. Christmas-tree ice cubes are ready to cool the punch.

HOLIDAY PUNCH

We have a few ice cube trays that make cubes shaped like Christmas trees. We've also seen trays of Santas, stars, and bells. Make cranberry-juice ice cubes for this punch.

1 cup water

1 cup sweetened cranberry juice*

2 750-ml. bottles cold pink champagne

1 lime, stuck with 40–60 whole cloves

¼ cup crème de cassis

Combine the water and juice and pour into ice cube trays; freeze at least 3 hours.

Combine the champagne, lime, and crème de cassis in a punch bowl. Add the ice cubes and ladle into glasses. *Serves 8–10.*

*If you want a dark-red ice cube, use 2 cups cranberry juice and no water.

❧ ❧

APPLES, ANGELS, CANDLES, AND LIGHT

As the days of Advent grow darker, we bring out the things of Christmas that help dispel the dark and lift the spirits of anyone who comes to visit.

Apples fill bowls and baskets throughout the barn. The large Red Delicious, the shining green Granny Smiths, and the tiny lady apples are all signs of welcome and simple abundance, and an inviting snack for anyone who wants one.

We enjoy making new white starched angels every season, as well as bringing out our well-loved wooden angels and placing them in familiar places in the 1836 Barn. Like old friends who come visiting, they nourish the soul. The angels were all hand-carved in the Erzgebirge, and one is an exact replica of one Ruth had as a child but lost in the destruction of the war. There's an angel orchestra, too, that comes out to sit on top of CD 199, one of Skitch's Steinway pianos. They're accompanied by a miniature street band and a coal miner's angel.

We collect candles throughout the year especially to use during Advent. They're placed all through the house and we burn more and more of them as Christmas week draws close. Some glow brightly in clusters of green glasses on a sideboard, some burn in solitary splendor in tall iron sconces. On any winter afternoon, Skitch can be seen moving slowly about the Great Room, meticulously lighting every candle. Some mornings, we'll light a candle at breakfast, and some nights, sitting in conversation with friends, we'll put one thick candle on a tin plate and pass a fresh sprig of evergreen through the flame—just enough to singe it and make it smoke. The spicy sweet smell of pine or juniper is inspiring.

FAR LEFT: *Our favorite rusted-metal candlesticks look like tree trunks and provide us with candles burning at different heights—a wonderful way to enjoy candlelight.*

❖73❖

FRUIT SOUPS AND
CHRISTMAS COOKIE PARTY

Peter Dubos, our Silo Gallery director, tapped into his Russian/Hungarian background and prepared these three remarkable fruit soups for us. After our cookie-baking party, we invited the bakers and packers to sample the soups, served with a cookie from the day's labor. You may also want to invite friends in for these festive soups after a concert or caroling, or even for late-afternoon tea.

> *Apricot—Mandarin*
> *Orange Soup*
>
> *Pear and Pineapple Soup*
>
> *Cherry Berry Soup*
>
> *Holiday Compote*
>
> *Basic Sugar Cookie*

FAR LEFT: *This Pear and Pineapple Soup is good served hot, cold, or at room temperature. A tree of dried branches is perfect for hanging the cookies, baked with a hole for that purpose.*

LEFT: *We plate and wrap the big cookies in cellophane. The smaller ones we pack in tins.*

APRICOT—MANDARIN ORANGE SOUP

You may also serve this soup garnished with a dollop of sour cream laced with peach liqueur, fresh peach or orange slices, or slivered dried apricots.

4 tablespoons (½ stick) unsalted butter
3 tablespoons flour
2 cups dried apricots, pureed
3 cups canned mandarin orange slices, with juice, pureed
2 cups freshly squeezed orange juice
2 cups whole baby carrots, peeled
1 cup canned peach slices, drained and pureed
¼ vanilla bean
½ cup honey
1½ cups carrot juice
Zest of half lemon
1 cup shredded sweetened coconut

Melt the butter in a saucepan over medium-low heat. Whisk in the flour and cook, whisking constantly, until mixture is golden. Stir in the remaining ingredients, except the coconut, one at a time and continue cooking until soup is hot and thick, about 1 hour. Do not boil. Remove the vanilla bean, ladle into individual bowls, and serve garnished with coconut. *Serves 6–8.*

ॐ ॐ

RIGHT: *The snowman is right at home next to the shredded-coconut "snow" that garnishes the Apricot—Mandarin Orange Soup.*

FAR RIGHT: *Fresh strawberries, quartered and with the stem left on, make a hearty garnish for the Cherry Berry Soup. The cookie makes it festive.*

PEAR AND PINEAPPLE SOUP

2 14-ounce jars or cans pears in juice
1 14-ounce can crushed pineapple in juice or 1 large fresh pineapple, peeled, cored, and chopped
4 tablespoons (½ stick) unsalted butter
3 tablespoons flour
1 tablespoon farina
2 cups unsweetened pineapple juice
1 cup apple juice
1 teaspoon minced fresh ginger root

Zest of 1 lemon
1 cup golden raisins
2 fresh pears, cored and thinly sliced
½ cup honey
Cinnamon sticks for garnish

Drain the pears, reserving the juice. Drain pineapple, discarding juice. Place pears and pineapple in the container of a food processor or blender and puree until smooth. Set aside.

Melt the butter in a medium saucepan over medium-low heat until it begins to brown. Whisk

in the flour and farina. Cook, whisking constantly, until golden brown. Add the pear-pineapple puree and stir in reserved pear juice, pineapple juice, apple juice, ginger, and lemon zest; cook 1 minute. Add the raisins, fresh pears, and honey. Continue cooking until the soup is hot and thick, about 1 hour. Do not boil.

Serve warm or chilled, ladled into bowls and garnished with a cinnamon stick. *Serves 6–8*.

❧ ❧

CHERRY BERRY SOUP

2 cups canned pitted cherries
4 tablespoons (½ stick) unsalted butter
3 tablespoons flour
1 cup dried blueberries or 1 cup frozen blueberries or
    strawberries, thawed
Zest of 1 lemon
½ cup honey
½ vanilla bean
2 cups cranberry juice, or more if necessary
¼ cup blanched slivered almonds, toasted

Drain the cherries and reserve the juice. Place cherries in the container of a food processor or blender; puree until smooth. Set aside.

Melt the butter in a saucepan over medium-low heat until it begins to brown. Whisk in the flour and cook, stirring constantly until golden. Stir in the pureed cherries, blueberries, reserved juice from the cherries, and lemon zest; cook 1 minute. Add the honey, vanilla bean, and cranberry juice. Simmer, but do not boil, until soup is hot and thick, about 1 hour. Add more cranberry juice if soup is too thick for your taste.

To serve, remove the vanilla bean, ladle into individual bowls, and garnish with toasted almonds. *Serves 6–8*.

❧ ❧

HOLIDAY COMPOTE

Here is a showy dessert. You can use any fruit, really—fresh, frozen, or canned. It's all in the presentation. Use your best fancy bowl.

1 cup seedless raisins
½ cup dark rum
¼ cup maple syrup (optional)
¼ cup lemon juice (optional)
4 14-ounce jars apricots, in juice
4 14-ounce jars pear halves, in juice
4 14-ounce jars pitted black cherries, in juice

Combine the raisins and rum in a medium bowl. Cover and let stand overnight. (Or, for a nonalcoholic soaking, combine the maple syrup and lemon juice and pour over the raisins.) Cover and let stand overnight.

Drain the apricots, pears, and cherries, reserving juice. Handle the fruit carefully, as it is fragile. Layer the fruit in a crystal bowl in the following order: apricots, ⅓ of the raisins, pears, ⅓ of the raisins, cherries, and remaining raisins. Add enough of the reserved juices to barely cover the fruit (do not allow the fruit to float).

To serve, spoon into small bowls or punch glasses. *Serves 20.*

❦❧

ABOVE: *This timesaving, easy-to-prepare dessert crowns a holiday table and may be served hot or cold.*

LEFT: *According to old English legend, Father Christmas rides atop a goat through the countryside, full of good cheer as he spreads the holiday spirit. This rendition, designed by Denise Calla for House of Hatten, happily guards a gift bottle of 1918 Armagnac Sempé, given to Skitch to honor the year of his birth.*

BASIC SUGAR COOKIE

This recipe will make six large (6-inch) cookies or 20 small (2½–3-inch) cookies. Double or triple recipe according to your needs.

¾ cup (1½ sticks) unsalted butter, softened
1 cup sugar
1 large egg
1 teaspoon vanilla extract
2 cups flour
½ teaspoon baking powder
½ teaspoon salt
Royal Icing (recipe follows)

Preheat the oven to 375° F.

Beat the butter and the sugar in the bowl of an electric mixer until creamy and pale yellow in color. Beat in the egg and vanilla. Gradually add the flour, baking powder, and salt. Beat until a soft dough forms. Shape into a ball and wrap in plastic wrap. Chill 3 hours.

Roll the dough out on a lightly floured surface to ¼-inch thickness (for large cookies) or ⅛-inch thickness (for small cookies). Cut out cookies with the cutters and place on ungreased cookie sheets. Bake until golden, about 10 minutes. Cool completely on a wire rack. (If cookies are to be used as ornaments, use a toothpick to make a hole in the top of the cookies while they are still hot from the oven.) Decorate with Royal Icing. *Makes 6 large or 20 small cookies.*

ROYAL ICING

3 egg whites
1 teaspoon cream of tartar
1 teaspoon flavored extract, such as vanilla, mint, almond, or maple
1 10-ounce box confectioners' sugar
Red, yellow, blue, green, and brown food coloring

Place all ingredients except the food coloring in the bowl of an electric mixer and beat on high speed for 3 to 5 minutes, until mixture is stiff.

Divide icing among several bowls and tint each bowl with a different color, leaving one bowl white. Leftover icing will keep 2 or 3 days in a zip-close bag in the refrigerator. *Makes 3 cups, enough to decorate 6 large or 20 small cookies.*

❧ ❧

LEFT: *A Santa Claus cookie jar doubles as a soup tureen. We had a snowman and a strawberry cookie jar at the party, too.*

AS THE SEASON GROWS

As the days of Advent pass and Christmas draws nearer, the pace and excitement of our lives pick up dramatically. For Skitch, it means a lot of traveling and performing in dozens of concert halls. As a very young musician, he was under contract with Metro-Goldwyn-Mayer and during the holidays played piano for another Metro contract player, Judy Garland, and later on for Bing Crosby and Rosemary Clooney. To this day, we get a taped Christmas card from Rosemary Clooney—a song and a personal message.

Still on the road at Christmastime, but no longer just at the keyboard, Skitch conducts Christmas concerts for symphony orchestras all over the country. Invariably, the programs include Ralph Blane's wonderful hit from *Meet Me in St. Louis*, "Have Yourself a Merry Little Christmas." Each time he conducts it, the memory of a very young Judy Garland sweeps over him. The recollection is so clear: She's performing the song (its first public performance) in a special concert for a large gathering of theater owners. Skitch is only a few feet away, accompanying her. She sings, and the traditionally critical and hard-to-please audience is riveted. As she holds the last note, letting it slowly fade, there isn't a dry eye in the house.

Now, for Skitch, it's the baton and symphonies of Christmas music—from Louisville, Kentucky, to the Florida Symphony in Tampa, Clearwater, and St. Petersburg, and then to Norfolk, Virginia. Before going on to each city, Skitch manages to snatch time to come

TOP LEFT: *Skitch conducts the New York Pops with the Harlem Boys Choir for a joyful holiday concert at Carnegie Hall.* TOP RIGHT: *In the early days, Camille and Mimi would pile into the Land Rover and go everywhere with us. Camille, in fact, was the Cupid at our first meeting. She was nestled in Ruth's travel bag at a rehearsal at the Colonial Theatre when Skitch, a dog lover, came over to say hello.* MIDDLE: *Judy Garland and Skitch rehearse for a radio broadcast of the "Bing Crosby Show." A loyal fan and friend of Judy's, Skitch took Ruth to hear Judy sing at the Palace in New York on his and Ruth's first date in 1956.* BOTTOM RIGHT: *Celebrating Christmas with skiing in Sugarbush, Vermont, was a Henderson tradition for many years.* BOTTOM LEFT: *Heidi is at the harp with her proud dad beside her in our brownstone in New York.*

◆ 81 ◆

ABOVE RIGHT: *Rosemary Clooney and Skitch share music and many memories. He never lets her forget that she's from Maysville, Kentucky!* TOP: *On stage at Bunkamura Hall in Tokyo, the New York Pops rings in the holidays, presenting the American sound as well as* Apollo, *a new work by the popular Japanese singer-composer Tanimura.* ABOVE: *This is Skitch's collection of English coronation cups, given to him by his colleagues in London.*

back to the farm. "I'm on my way in for a home-cooked meal," comes the call from an airport somewhere. For one or two days, Skitch gets to see the kids, take them to town for a concert, have that home-cooked meal, and give in to the irresistible smells of spices and evergreens that fill the house before he heads back to work. Closer to Christmas, the music gets closer to home. There are three performances at Carnegie Hall with the New York Pops and the Harlem Boys Choir and more concerts with the New Haven Symphony in Connecticut. Then it's back to Carnegie Hall to rehearse for the New York Pops concert tour to Japan that rings in the new year.

When Ruth was a child, the approaching third week of Advent meant for her that all the great spicy smells of cinnamon, apple, and pine, plus candlelight and music, would spill out of everybody's home and mingle with the sights and smells of the open marketplace—the *Weihnachtsmarkt*—set up in the town square. There were *hundreds* of booths—simple wooden structures with canvas roofs and rough-hewn shelves and tables. Little metal stoves kept each booth warm. Lanterns hung from beams above, swayed in the night winds, and cast dancing light on all the gifts to tempt the shoppers.

Glassblowers made sleigh bells, delicate reindeer, and angels. There were handcarved angels, Santas, and a special coal-mining angel—really a candle holder in which the heat of the flame caused a hammer to strike a bell. There were handmade dolls, little men made of dried prunes and apples, puppets, and cuckoo clocks.

The smells were thick and intoxicating—burning candle wax, chestnuts roasting in large tin pans, melted chocolate poured into molds and then hardening into Santas in front of your eyes, burnt almonds, and the sweet smell of spun-sugar angel hair.

Music welled out from endless music boxes, some featuring solo voices, a choir of children, or just the glockenspiel. There were small musical instruments too—child-size recorders, violins, harmonicas, triangles.

And apples! Plain, roasted on the little stoves, or candied with caramel. The glorious cold night was everywhere too. It was a rare and wonderful opportunity for Ruth to stay up late—a special treat in honor of Christmas.

Now, instead of the outdoor *Weihnachtsmarkt* of her childhood, Ruth creates her own indoor Christmas marketplace in the Silo Store and Gallery. It's a very busy time for her and the staff. The tables, walls, beams, and shelves are laden with pottery bowls and dishes, brightly colored linens, glassware, baskets, gleaming gadgets, and cutlery. There are books on every cuisine and culinary topic, jars of gourmet delicacies—jams, chutney and preserves, bags of cookies, and tins of cakes. In the gallery, the majestic tree stands decorated with ornaments and bows, and every bit of wall and pinewood floor is filled with handmade crafts, ornaments, and gifts. The comforting smells of cinnamon and pine and the interesting textures of handcarved wood and woven tapestries are all there, housed in the rough-hewn wood barn.

Christmas shoppers stream in during the day and, to accommodate everybody, the store keeps late hours on several nights before Christmas. One very popular night is Men's Night. From 5:00 to 9:00 p.m., men only are invited to cocktails, hors d'oeuvres, and shopping to fulfill the wish lists of their wives and girlfriends. The men love it, even though women have recently been invited to crash the event.

TOP: *We are greeted by Lady Bird Johnson at the White House, where Skitch had performed for the holiday season.*

ABOVE: *Each year in early November, the Silo Gallery turns into a Christmas wonderland.*

Third Week of Advent

GOING TO THE BIG CITY

As much as we love living on the farm, when it comes to be the third Sunday of Advent, memories from our Christmases in New York draw us back in and we make a trip. Keiran and Kythera, Hans and Sandra join us. We start out after a hearty midday meal and allow plenty of time to drive all over town. First we stop at Lord & Taylor to look at the animated scenes in the store windows. Then it's a drive uptown into our old neighborhood on East 61st Street, the Treadwell Farm district, which is now a landmark area. During our years living there, at Christmastime, Skitch would lead a two-block carol sing. All our neighbors decorated their front doors, windows, and entryways with huge evergreen wreaths and thick garlands. The carolers stood singing at the bottom of the stoop. "God rest ye merry, gentlemen, let nothing you dismay . . ." Skitch remembers that by the time we got to "O tidings of comfort and joy, comfort and joy . . ." the big brownstone doors would open and in we would go for warm drinks and food. We drive slowly by our old brownstone. The kids peer up at the big parlor-floor windows. We describe the tree we had there each year in the living room, under a thirty-five-foot vaulted ceiling.

Then, as night falls, it's on to Rockefeller Center to watch the thousands of lights brighten the great tree as skaters twirl on the ice rink below. When we lived in the city, frequent trips to this rink and to the Wollman Rink in Central Park were a ritual. Hans, in fact, started skating before he was two years old. He was so small that we had to have his skates custom-made. We still have them. They hang

Pea and Potato Stew

Christmas Croutons

FAR LEFT: *With Hans riding in the basket, Ruth would bicycle across town to Central Park to enjoy skating and sunshine.*

ABOVE LEFT: *On opening night at Daly's Dandelion in 1967, Skitch is joined by, from left, New York restaurateurs Molly and Charlie Berns from the 21 Club, Michael Pearman from Michael's Pub, Jan Mitchell from Lüchow's, Vincent Sardi from Sardi's, and Johnny Nicholson from Cafe Nicholson. Mayor John Lindsay was there too, helping Skitch tend bar.*

ABOVE RIGHT: *Here we are at our wedding breakfast at Lüchow's in 1958.*

on the hall coat tree in the barn and look almost like antiques—high-laced black leather with old-fashioned wooden skate guards.

For all of us, then, it's an informal dinner. In days gone by we would plan a dinner at Lüchow's on 14th Street—the wonderful old German restaurant with carved wooden walls and ceilings, stained-glass windows, and crystal chandeliers. At Christmas, it was filled with music, an enormous magical tree, and gifts for every child who came to dinner. It was a high-spirited and joyous gathering place that reflected the life of Jan Mitchell, the creative owner. We're sad now that Lüchow's is gone; it can never be replaced. Perhaps it should have been declared a landmark too so that our grandchildren could have shared it with their children.

After dinner, we go to the New York State Theater at Lincoln Center to take in *The Nutcracker Suite* ballet. Afterward, we treat the kids to a sweet of another kind at Rumpelmayer's on Central Park South. Of course, we buy bags of hot roasted chestnuts from the vendor on the corner. We'll eat some and save some so the fabulous aroma can permeate the car on the ride home.

ABOVE: *We lived at 234 East 61st Street until we moved to the farm. Daly's was on the corner, a half block away at 61st and Third Avenue. Our block association was a tightly knit group—almost like a small-town community with strong neighborhood spirit. We met each month in one house or another and we planted the block with trees and daffodils in the spring. We cooked in our gardens in summer and decorated our houses at Christmas. When we did a little research and discovered that we all lived on what used to be Treadwell Farm, we applied for and won landmark status for the neighborhood.* ABOVE RIGHT: *Hans and Heidi are ready for a Christmas party. They excitedly run down the four-story staircase.*

ABOVE MIDDLE: *Skitch at the Steinway in our living room, which was the scene of many New York after-concert parties—memories go back as far as Maestro Stokowski's American Symphony Orchestra.*

ABOVE: *Mayor Lindsay and Skitch celebrate at Daly's Dandelion. When we closed the restaurant, the antique bar and massive brass railings, turn-of-the-century light fixtures, and the stained-glass Daly's sign found a happy second life at Laney's, a restaurant in Manchester Center, Vermont*

PEA AND POTATO STEW

This is really a variation on good old-fashioned pea soup, made a little more thick and hearty with potatoes and carrots. We often cook it the day before and merely warm it in a large crock for an easy and early dinner.

2½ quarts water
24 ounces (4 cups) dried peas
2 large onions, peeled and roughly chopped
1 medium ham hock or ham bone
3 large potatoes, peeled and sliced ⅛- to ¼-inch thick
6 medium carrots, peeled and sliced ¼-inch thick
1 pound kielbasa, cut in ¾-inch-thick pieces
Salt and freshly ground pepper
Christmas Croutons (recipe follows)

Put the water in a large stockpot and bring to a boil. Add the peas and boil 2 minutes. Remove from heat and let stand for ½ hour. Add the onions and ham hock. Heat to boiling, reduce heat, and simmer over low heat for 1 hour. Remove the ham hock. Add the potatoes and carrots; simmer until the carrots are just tender, about 20 minutes, stirring frequently. Add the kielbasa; simmer until warmed through, about 5 minutes. Season to taste and pour into a 4-quart serving crock or bowl. Serve with Christmas Croutons. *Serves 6–10.*

✑ ✑

ABOVE RIGHT: *This board from Daly's Dandelion makes a perfect serving tray for a bowl of soup. We left the croutons in their copper cookie cutters to add a little glitter and shine.*

FAR RIGHT: *Here, we've topped our bread wreath with a few fresh pine boughs. Day or night, the holidays invite the use of candles.*

CHRISTMAS CROUTONS

We used fancy cookie cutters to make these croutons, then later gave the cutters away as ornaments.

12–15 slices dark bread, crusts removed
6 tablespoons (¾ stick) unsalted butter

Using a 2- or 2½-inch Christmas tree–shaped cookie cutter (or any other Christmas-theme cutter), cut shapes out of bread slices.

Melt 2 tablespoons of the butter in a large skillet over medium-high heat. Add a few of the trees and sauté until toasted, about 4 minutes on each side. Transfer to a plate. Add more butter to the skillet and repeat process until all trees are toasted. *Makes 24 croutons.*

✑ ✑

THE GINGERBREAD HOUSES

Each year for years and years now, Sandy Daniels, the director of the Silo Cooking School, has conducted a gingerbread-house class for parents and children. The parent-child team does everything together: makes the dough, rolls it out onto cookie sheets, cuts out house pieces, bakes and designs the house. Sometimes it's an older brother or sister who teams up with the little one. At first we offered just one class for the Christmas season. The following year we had to add another to accommodate everyone who wanted to participate. Now we offer four classes, but if we had the time, we could fill six or more. This last Christmas season, we had a very special alumna return for another season—a woman who first came to the class as a little girl with *her* mother had returned to build a house with her own little girl. The kids and the parents love the experience together.

There is never a set pattern for decorating, and not one house looks like any of the others. The point for the students is to make the most mouth-watering and deliciously tempting fantasy house that they can. And they do.

♦91♦

FAR LEFT: *At our Silo gingerbread-house class, each parent-child team builds a house and takes it home. Some houses are simple, and some are completely covered with candy decorations selected from a variety set out in bowls. Whatever emerges will be truly individual.*

BELOW LEFT: *Choosing the right candy decorations is important. For every one that goes on the house, one goes into the mouth.*

BELOW: *Daren Daniels, a young master baker, adds an icing trim to his house with a pastry bag.*

LEFT: *Children-adult teams consider carefully as they look over all the decorating possibilities.*

RIGHT: *The mom on one team holds a wall steady as the royal icing "cement" sets firm. Meanwhile, she and her daughter raise the other wall.*

FAR RIGHT: *Intense creative juices go into making this fantasy roof!*

◆92◆ Here is Sandy's step-by-step organizational plan for building your Gingerbread House. Kids are very creative when all the tools are organized and ready for them. Pace yourself! You needn't do all of the project in one day. If you're working with children, you'll notice they love to look forward to the next day's project. Gather the ingredients one day. Make the dough another day. Bake the pieces another day. Build the house another day.

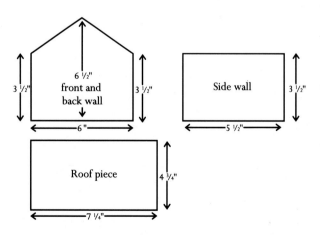

EQUIPMENT

Disposable or regular pastry bags and tips

Small muffin tins or empty egg cartons

13–14-inch very stiff cardboard circle, covered with foil

15x18-inch cookie sheet with one open end

Rolling pin

Sharp knife and cookie cutters

Cardboard templates for house walls (see directions below)

INGREDIENTS

2 batches Royal Icing (see recipe, page 79)

2–3 8-ounce bags M&Ms

2–3 8¼-ounce bags cinnamon red hots

Pretzel nuggets

2 11-ounce bags gumdrops of various sizes and colors

2 14-ounce bags chocolate kisses

4 2-ounce rolls Necco wafers

2 foil-wrapped chocolate Santas, about 1½–2 inches tall

2 10-ounce bags miniature colored marshmallows

2 10-ounce bags large marshmallows

2 4-ounce bags gummy bears
Colored sugar sprinkles (red and green sugar crystals) or
   confetti
12 rolls Life Savers of various flavors and colors
3 5-ounce packages red licorice sticks

1. Gather all equipment and ingredients listed
above.

2. Make 6 templates for house pieces. You will
need 3 sheets of cardboard, 8½x11 inches each, to
build 1 house. Using a ruler, draw 2 of each of the
shapes diagrammed at left on cardboard. You will
then have 2 side walls, 2 roof panels, and 1 front
and 1 back wall.

3. Make the gingerbread dough. If you and
your children are going to work together, it's a
very good idea to make the dough one or two
days before you bake and build your house.

7–8 cups flour
1½ teaspoons salt
1½ teaspoons baking soda

8 teaspoons ground ginger
4 teaspoons cinnamon
2 teaspoons ground cloves
2 teaspoons freshly grated nutmeg
1 teaspoon ground cardamom
1½ cups (3 sticks) unsalted butter, softened
2¼ cups sugar
1½ cups molasses
½ cup water

Combine 4 cups of the flour, the salt, the baking soda, and the spices in a large bowl. In the
bowl of an electric mixer, beat the butter and sugar
until light and creamy. Beat in the molasses and the
water. Gradually add the flour mixture and beat
until well blended. Add the remaining flour, one
cup at a time, until the mixture forms a firm, soft
dough. Shape the dough into a ball and flatten into
a rectangle. Wrap in plastic and chill in the refrigerator at least 3 hours or overnight. This dough
will keep at least 3 days in the refrigerator.

4. Cut and bake Gingerbread House walls and roof. Preheat oven to 350° F.

Roll out the dough onto an open-ended 15x18-inch cookie sheet to about ¼-inch thickness, filling the sheet. Then, using a sharp knife, trim the dough to leave a ½-inch space between the dough and the edge of the sheet.

Lightly dust the cardboard templates with flour and arrange them to fit on the dough. Using a sharp knife, cut the dough around the template. You should then have 6 house pieces cut into the dough. Remove any extra dough between the shapes and reserve. (These can be cut with your favorite cookie cutter for gingerbread people or reindeer, etc.)

Bake until firm to the touch, about 15 minutes. Remove from oven and, while pieces are still hot, trim along sides with a sharp knife to make sure you get clean edges. Place the pieces on a rack to cool. When the pieces are completely cool, begin building your house. You can also wrap each piece in plastic wrap and refrigerate or freeze until ready to build.

Makes 1 large house.

5. Build your house. Place the decorating ingredients listed on pages 92–93 in muffin tins or egg cartons to keep them organized and separated.

Lay out baked and cooled gingerbread walls on the cardboard circle as diagrammed below:

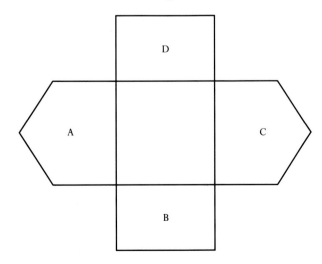

ABOVE: *Daren Daniels and our granddaughter, Kythera, use the same techniques they learned for the large gingerbread house to build and decorate miniature gingerbread houses, which will make an appearance on our Christmas table.*
RIGHT: *Disposable plastic pastry bags with a small hole cut in the tip make for easy decoration and fast cleanup. Note that the top is twist-tied closed to prevent spilling.*

A is the front-door wall, C is the back-door wall, B and D are side walls. Roof pieces are not pictured.

Fill a pastry bag fitted with a star-shaped tip with Royal Icing (if children are doing the icing, close off the open end with a rubber band).

Stand Wall A up in its place in the layout and pipe icing along the inside baseline, coating both cookie and cardboard. Hold firm. Pipe icing along the outside baseline of Wall A, coating both cookie and cardboard. Hold firm for a few seconds, then brace with a can. It should stand easily on its own. Next, pipe icing down the left edge of Wall A. Stand up Wall B to meet the iced edge of Wall A at a right angle. Hold firm for a few seconds. Pipe icing along inside baseline of Wall B and hold firm a few seconds. Pipe icing along outside baseline of Wall B. Brace with a can. Now, pipe icing down right edge of Wall A and stand up Wall D to meet the iced edge of Wall A at a right angle. Hold firm for a few seconds. Then pipe icing along inside

baseline of Wall D and hold firm a few seconds. Pipe icing along outside baseline of Wall D. Hold firm a few seconds, then brace with a can. You should now have the 3 pieces—front wall and 2 side walls—standing and glued with icing to each other.

Pipe icing down both edges and along the inside baseline of Wall C. Then stand it upright to meet Walls B and D. Hold firm a few seconds. Pipe icing along outside baseline of Wall C. Hold firm a few seconds.

To attach roof pieces, pipe icing along the right roof edge of Wall A, along the top edge of Wall D, and along the right roof edge of Wall C. Lay the roof piece so that front, back, and bottom edges extend slightly beyond house walls. Hold firm until set, a few seconds. Repeat on the opposite side with the other roof piece.

Tips for Decorating Your House

Using a pastry bag fitted with a small tip, apply dabs of Royal Icing to the house and attach candy decorations to the icing. Here are some ideas: Arrange overlapping M&Ms on the roof for shingles. Necco wafers also make great roof shingles. Use chocolate kisses for windows or use red licorice sticks to outline windows. Use tiny gumdrops to outline the front door. Hang a Life Saver wreath on the door. Larger gumdrops or miniature colored marshmallows can be used to outline the roof. A large marshmallow makes a great chimney: place a foil-wrapped chocolate Santa next to it. Pipe extra icing on the "ground" around the house to create a snow-covered yard and sprinkle it with colored sugar sprinkles. Pretzel nuggets make a fine fence.

Heartbreak Alert!

Children love this Gingerbread House process but invariably they drop things, break house pieces, spill icing, and knock over decorations. To guard against heartbreak, make extra house pieces if you can. Have extra decorating candy available: we have noticed that for every sweet decoration that goes on the house, one also goes in the mouth!

Remember! Pace yourself.

Allow 10 minutes to set firm.

Decorate as desired by first piping a dab of icing on the house, then attaching the decorations.

☙ ❧

PEACE FOR ALL, ALL CREATURES
GREAT AND SMALL

T his was the theme of the 1992 Deck the Halls Show, which opened our Gallery of Gifts at the Silo. The show is always special to us because 150 artists contribute original one-of-a-kind ornaments to be sold to benefit our New Milford Hospital. Not only do the artists donate their work, but the local newspapers give us free advertising space, vendors donate gourmet foods, restaurants cater the reception, and the Silo staff members volunteer extra time. Each year we have made enough money to help purchase a new piece of equipment for the hospital.

Peace for All, All Creatures Great and Small turned out to be quite a powerful theme. It stimulated the artists to produce remarkable animal ornaments. Then the theme began to flow over into all aspects of the farm. Animals began to show up on wreaths and packages. Diana Mihaltse, an artisan whose work we often feature at the Silo, made extraordinary animal ornaments from tin, patterned after American quilt designs. We captured a few for Heidi's tree, which our grandsons Will and Sam enjoyed during their stay in the 1836 House. Then we used the tin ornaments as templates for large gingerbread creatures.

FAR LEFT: *A collection of favorite teddy bears and a Santa are strategically seated around the All Creatures Great and Small tree in the 1836 House. It will be safe (for the moment) from toddlers Will and Sam.*

❖97❖

GINGERBREAD ORNAMENTS

You can make templates for these animal-shaped cookie ornaments by tracing pictures of ducks, pigs, horses, cows, and other animals onto cardboard and cutting them out. Our ornaments were 10 inches long because we wanted big animals on the trees.

7–8 cups flour
1½ teaspoons salt
1½ teaspoons baking soda
8 teaspoons ground ginger
4 teaspoons cinnamon
2 teaspoons ground cloves
2 teaspoons freshly grated nutmeg
1 teaspoon ground cardamom
1½ cups (3 sticks) unsalted butter, softened
1¼ cups sugar
1½ cups light molasses

Combine 4 cups of the flour, the salt, the baking soda, and the spices in a large bowl. In the bowl of an electric mixer, beat the butter and sugar until light and creamy. Beat in the molasses. Gradually add the flour mixture and beat until well blended. Add the remaining flour, one cup at a time, until the mixture forms a firm, soft dough. Divide the dough in half and form each half into a brick. Wrap in plastic wrap and chill in the refrigerator at least 3 hours or overnight. This dough will keep at least 3 days in the refrigerator. Preheat oven to 350° F.

Roll out one portion of the chilled dough onto rimless or open-ended 15x18-inch cookie sheet to about ¼-inch thickness, filling the sheet. Then, using a sharp knife, trim the dough to leave a ½-inch space between the dough and the edge of the sheet.

Place an animal template on the dough and, using a sharp knife, cut the dough around the template. Repeat with as many shapes as you can. Remove dough between the shapes and reserve for another use.

Bake 15 minutes. Remove from the oven and, while ornaments are still hot, trim along the sides of the shapes with a sharp knife to make sure edges are clean. Cut a hole with a sharp pointed knife where you intend to hang the ornament. Place the ornaments on a rack to cool, then store until tree-trimming time. Decorate or leave unadorned, as we did. *Makes 4 10-inch ornaments.*

FAR LEFT: *We load the tree with Diana Mihaltse's painted-tin ornaments, our gingerbread animals, and an heirloom garland made by Mary Ann Sabados from upholstery rope and pieces of beloved old clothes we could not bear to throw away.*

LEFT: *Our favorite hand-carved Santa is catching the afternoon sun on the fireplace in the 1836 House.*

ABOVE: *The farm-animal-shaped cookies are cooled, strung with twine, and ready to be hung on a wreath or tree—or, to the delight of the kids, eaten!*

LEFT: *Out come the horses from Heidi's childhood—Big Freddy and Little Freddy. A brand-new soft Santa sculpture sits perched on a little child's chair.*

SWEET TREES

These are easy to make and fun to give. If you're involved with charity functions, or hosting a children's party, these make great centerpieces or door prizes. You could also bring one along as a house gift for a friend or neighbor. Since most of the adults we know become more childlike during Christmastime, their eyes light up just as much as the kids' do when they see a sweet tree.

A sweet tree is just one idea for a theme tree. Any kind of tree or branch can be decorated with small toy cars, cookies in dinosaur shapes, soft-sculpture birds, hand-blown glass, colored bells, antique buttons. Just imagine!

For the baker, hang the branches with cookie cutters. Hundreds are available depicting all aspects of life—tractors, cars, trains, tools, houses, the entire animal and plant kingdoms. Bake some cookie ornaments too to mix in with the cookie cutters.

For the adventurous cook, hang the branches with small gadgets—a zester, peeler, garlic press, nutmeg grater. Tie them on with cooking twine and leave the roll of twine on the bottom.

Cover a Styrofoam cone with burlap and, for your nut-loving friends, use a glue gun to make a tree of different kinds of nuts—hazelnuts, walnuts, pecans. Paint a few of them silver or gold or leave the tree all natural.

> *Chocolate Kisses and Cherry Ball Tree*
>
> *Peppermint Tree*
>
> *Pinwheels and Gummy Bear Tree*
>
> *Chocolate Truffle Tree*

FAR LEFT: *Bare branches are the perfect home for our twelve days of Christmas theme-tree ornaments. The sweet peppermint, pinwheel, and chocolate kisses trees make wonderful centerpieces and gifts.*

❖ 101 ❖

CHOCOLATE KISSES AND CHERRY BALL TREE

EQUIPMENT

Pastry bag and star-shaped tip
12–14-inch-high Styrofoam cone
8–10-inch cardboard circle

INGREDIENTS

2 batches Royal Icing (see recipe, page 79)
4 dozen silver-wrapped chocolate kisses, about 2
   14-ounce bags
2 dozen unwrapped cherry sour balls (or red jawbreakers)
2 3-inch candy canes

Fill a pastry bag fitted with star-shaped tip with half of the Royal Icing. (Cover remaining icing tightly and keep in refrigerator.)

♦ 102 ♦ Place the cone on the cardboard circle and pipe icing around the base of the cone to secure. Working quickly, pipe stars to cover the cone, creating a surface of icing stars. Let dry 5 minutes. Press the kisses one at a time into icing stars, leaving spaces between kisses, until all the kisses are on the tree. Place in a safe place and let dry overnight.

Rewhip the refrigerated icing and spoon it into a pastry bag fitted with star-shaped tip. Pipe stars in the spaces between the kisses. Fill in randomly with cherry sour balls by pressing them into fresh icing stars. Pipe frosting on very top and affix candy canes. Let stand in a safe place until dry.

৩ ২

PEPPERMINT TREE

EQUIPMENT

Pastry bag and star-shaped tip
12–14-inch-high Styrofoam cone
8–10-inch cardboard circle

INGREDIENTS

2 batches Royal Icing (see recipe, page 79)
2 dozen red-and-white peppermint candies
2 dozen green-and-white peppermint candies
2 dozen chocolate chips
2 dozen fresh candy spearmint leaves

Fill a pastry bag fitted with the large star tip with half of the Royal Icing. (Cover remaining icing tightly and keep in refrigerator.) Place the cone on the cardboard circle and pipe icing around the base of the cone to secure. Working quickly, pipe stars to cover the cone, creating a surface of icing stars. Let dry 5 minutes. Press the peppermint candies one at a time into icing stars, leaving spaces in between, until all the candies are on the tree. Place in a safe place and let dry overnight.

Re-whip the refrigerated icing and spoon it into a pastry bag fitted with the large star tip. Pipe stars in the spaces between the candies. Fill in randomly with candied chocolate chips and spearmint leaves by pressing them into the fresh icing stars. Let stand in a safe place until dry.

৩ ২

RIGHT: *This tree in the Main House is decorated with hand-blown glass ornaments from Bavaria, made according to a tradition that has thrived for hundreds of years. They break easily, but we take good care of them because they are so much fun to collect.*

Pinwheels and Gummy Bear Tree

EQUIPMENT

Pastry bag and large star tip
10–12-inch-high Styrofoam cone
8–10-inch cardboard circle

INGREDIENTS

6 cups flour
1 teaspoon salt
6 teaspoons baking powder
2 cups (4 sticks) unsalted butter, softened
4 cups sugar
4 eggs, lightly beaten
2 teaspoons peppermint flavoring
Red food coloring
Royal Icing (see recipe, page 79)
3 dozen gummy bears
3 candy canes, each 2½ inches long

Combine the flour, salt, and baking powder in a large bowl. In the bowl of an electric mixer, beat the butter and sugar together until light and creamy. Add the eggs and peppermint, beating well after each addition. Gradually beat in the flour mixture until the dough is smooth and elastic. Divide the dough in half. Add red food coloring to one half and mix well. Shape both portions into bricks, cover with plastic wrap, and chill at least 3 hours or overnight.

Roll out the red dough on a lightly floured surface into a rectangle ⅛-inch thick. Roll out the white dough in the same way. Cut each rectangle in half horizontally. Gently lift half of the red dough and place it on half of the white dough. Repeat with the other half. Roll each red-and-white strip jelly-roll fashion, starting from the short ends. Wrap rolls in plastic wrap and chill 1 hour.

Preheat the oven to 400° F. Lightly grease a cookie sheet. Cut the rolls into approximately 40 ⅛- to ¼-inch slices and place cookies on prepared sheet. Bake until lightly golden, about 8 minutes. While the cookies are still hot from the oven, use a toothpick to make a hole through the top of each. Cool on a rack.

To assemble the tree, fill a pastry bag fitted with the large star tip with Royal Icing. Place the cone on the cardboard circle and pipe icing around the base of the cone to secure.

Attach the cookies to the cone by inserting a toothpick through the hole in each cookie and piercing the toothpick into the Styrofoam. The cookie should lie flat against the cone. Cover the exposed end of the toothpick with a gummy bear. Continue this process until the entire cone is covered with cookies. Pipe enough icing at the top to hold the candy canes as a top decoration. Hold firm a few seconds until set.

❧

CHOCOLATE TRUFFLE TREE

For this tree, we used our Connecticut neighbor Ruedi Hauser's chocolate truffles, chosen by *The New York Times* as some of the best. You can make any size tree, but here is our step-by-step plan for a tree 8 inches in diameter at the base and 12 inches high.

1 pound couverture (professional-quality chocolate, available from specialty confectioners)
108 chocolate truffles (about 3½ pounds), or about 92 dark chocolate truffles and 16 white chocolate truffles
Confectioners' sugar (optional)

Place the couverture in a glass bowl and place in the microwave. Microwave on low for 15 seconds at a time until chocolate is pliable but not liquid. This is going to be the "glue" you will use to build your tree of truffles. If, during the process, the chocolate becomes too hard to work with, simply microwave again to make it pliable.

On a plate or cardboard round approximately 8 inches in diameter, make the first base circle of 18 truffles. Using a small spoon, place a small amount of melted couverture on one side of a truffle and press it gently to the side of another until they stick together. Repeat until all 18 truffles forming the base ring are "glued" together. Let dry 1 hour.

Meanwhile, on a sheet of wax paper, construct the next ring, which will have 16 truffles. Affix the truffles together using the melted couverture as before and let dry 1 hour. When it is dry and the base ring is dry, carefully add small dollops of melted couverture to the tops of the truffles in the base ring. Lift the 16-truffle ring from the wax paper (it will hold together if you lift it very carefully and hold it level). Place the smaller ring on top of the base ring and let stand until the melted couverture begins to harden, about 5 minutes. Apply the

next 10 rings in the same manner (see the ring sizes below)—assembling each on wax paper, affixing the truffles together with melted couverture, allowing the ring to dry 1 hour, applying melted chocolate to the lower ring, placing the smaller ring on top, and allowing a few minutes to dry. Remember, each ring needs an hour to dry before placing it on the tree.

Dust with confectioners' sugar (snow) if you like.

Ring 3—14 truffles; Ring 4—12 truffles; Ring 5—10 truffles; Ring 6—8 truffles; Ring 7— 7 truffles; Ring 8—6 truffles; Ring 9—5 truffles; Ring 10—4 truffles; Ring 11—3 truffles; Top—1 truffle.

ABOVE: *The edible barley-sugar plates are made by candy maker Dorothy Timberlake of Eaton Center, New Hampshire. With a collection of more than three thousand antique candy molds, Ms. Timberlake creates old-fashioned candy in hundreds of fantasy shapes.* RIGHT: *To devour the tree, here's a hint: Use a grapefruit knife or spoon to loosen the truffles. Eat from the top down.*

RUTH STEINWAY'S NEW ENGLAND FISH CHOWDER DINNER

The people close to her knew Ruth Steinway as Utie, and she was the matriarch of the Steinway family. Skitch met Utie and her husband, Theodore Steinway, during his early radio days in New York and quickly became an adopted member of this great family. All of his professional life, Skitch has been devoted to the Steinway piano. The first time Skitch introduced Ruth to Utie, Ruth was as nervous as if she were meeting an in-law-to-be. But all fear was dispelled as Utie welcomed Ruth with great affection and warmth into the Steinway clan. From that moment on, Utie's family and ours became as close as any two can be. Utie insisted on hosting Ruth and Skitch's wedding breakfast at Lüchow's. John Steinway, one of Utie's sons, became Hans's godfather, and Betty Chapin, Utie's daughter, is godmother to Heidi.

For almost thirty years, our family spent summers in the boathouse at the Steinway residence at Long Pond, in Plymouth, Massachusetts, and enjoyed sharing life in abundance with Utie. She was a joyful cook and generous entertainer, always setting a table for more than expected. After a big holiday feast, it was tradition at the Steinways' to remove the plates and have the youngest child present walk down the center of the long, long table. Depending on the child, the walk would be timid or joyful, giddy or proud.

This meal makes us remember the big heart and spirit of Utie Steinway. The chowder is her recipe, given to us by Betty Chapin, who watched her make it many times. It is simple, elegant, and delicious—perfect for special friends to enjoy during the holidays.

Ruth Steinway's New England Fish Chowder

Pan-Roasted Peppers

Monkey Bread

Äpfel im Schlafrock mit Himbeergeist
APPLES WRAPPED IN PASTRY WITH RASPBERRY SCHNAPPS

◆107◆

FAR LEFT: *Hand-thrown fish-shaped pottery is heated before we fill it with the steaming chowder. Wilton Armetale chargers protect the oak table. Monkey bread is baked in small pots.* ABOVE: *Ruth Steinway presides at our wedding breakfast.*

RUTH STEINWAY'S NEW ENGLAND FISH CHOWDER

This is a rich, brothy chowder that is very satisfying. We poached the whole fish, then used the poaching liquid to make the chowder. Your European friends and guests will be delighted by the salt pork, capers, and cornichons served on the side—a culinary custom from their part of the world.

7–8 pound haddock with head and tail, cleaned and gutted, or 3 pounds haddock or cod fillet cut into 2-inch pieces, at room temperature

POACHING LIQUID

1 medium onion, peeled and quartered

1 leek, washed and halved lengthwise

2 bay leaves

1 stalk celery, with leaves

2 large sprigs fresh lovage or celery leaves

1 medium carrot, scrubbed

3 sprigs fresh dill

1 pound salt pork, diced

6 small onions, peeled and thinly sliced

3 sprigs winter savory or celery leaves

3 pounds potatoes (about 6 large), peeled and sliced

6 medium carrots, scrubbed and cut into ¼-inch slices

2 cups milk

Freshly chopped chives for garnish

3 tablespoons capers

8 cornichons (optional)

To poach a whole fish, stuff the cavity of the fish with all the poaching-liquid ingredients. Place the stuffed whole fish in a large fish poacher. Secure the fish to a rack with cheesecloth ties. Cover with water and heat to a low simmer. Continue simmering 10 minutes per 1-inch thickness of fish (ours took 30 minutes for a 3-inch-thick fish). Remove the fish and allow to cool; then remove the head, tail, skin, and bones. Cut or break into 2-inch pieces and set aside. Strain poaching liquid and reserve.

To poach fish fillets, place the fish and poaching-liquid ingredients on a steamer rack in a stockpot. Add enough water to cover and heat to a low simmer. Continue simmering 10 minutes per 1-inch thickness of fish. Remove the fish immediately with a slotted spoon and allow to cool. Strain poaching liquid and reserve.

Cook the salt pork in a soup pot over medium-high heat until light brown and crisp. Remove half the pork; drain on paper towels and set aside. Add the onions to the remaining salt pork and cook until the onions are translucent, about 5 minutes. Add the savory and potatoes. Cook another 5 minutes, stirring gently but constantly. Add the carrots and reserved poaching liquid. Heat to boiling; then

PAN-ROASTED PEPPERS

These peppers are very colorful. They make the table look festive, and the flavor is irresistible. If you have lots of leftovers, as we usually do, you can chop the remaining roasted peppers into smaller pieces and pack them into sterilized canning jars. Fill the jar with olive oil to cover (or half olive and half hot-pepper oil). Seal and process in a hot water bath.

2 tablespoons hot-pepper oil or olive oil
3 large green bell peppers, seeded and quartered
3 large red bell peppers, seeded and quartered

Heat the oil in a large skillet until hot but not smoking. Add the peppers; toss with tongs to coat well and cook until slightly charred and barely tender, about 8 minutes. *Serves 6 to 10.*

reduce heat. Continue simmering until the carrots are tender, about 8 minutes.

Remove the savory. Add the milk and fish pieces. Simmer until warmed through. To serve, ladle into pre-warmed soup bowls and sprinkle with chopped chives. Pass reserved salt pork, capers, and cornichons on the side. *Serves 6 to 10.*

ABOVE: *Our round oak pedestal table seats six and has wheels on the bottom, which allows us to move it anywhere in the Great Room. Here it's in front of our hunt-scene screen.*

RIGHT: *Red and green peppers create a vivid centerpiece as well as adding spicy flavor to the meal.*

MONKEY BREAD

This is a pull-apart bread, probably so named because of its silly look. Sometimes it's also called bubble bread, and it is perfect for dipping and dunking in the rich broth of the chowder.

¾ cup warm water

1 tablespoon sugar

1 packet (¼ ounce) active dry yeast

3 cups milk, scalded and cooled to 110° F.

1 cup (2 sticks) unsalted butter, softened

6–8 cups sifted flour

2 teaspoons salt

3 large eggs, lightly beaten, at room temperature

Combine the water and sugar in a large bowl. Sprinkle the surface with yeast and stir. Let sit until mixture begins to bubble, about 5 minutes. Stir in the milk and ⅓ of the butter.

Combine 6 cups of the flour and the salt in the bowl of an electric mixer fitted with a paddle. Add the milk mixture and eggs and beat until blended. Attach the dough hook and knead, adding more flour as needed, until the dough is smooth and elastic, about 10 minutes. Place in a large, lightly oiled bowl. Cover with a clean damp towel and place in a warm, draft-free place until doubled in size, about 1½ hours.

Punch the dough down and knead slightly in the bowl. Melt the remaining ⅔ of the butter. Roll the dough out on a lightly floured surface to 1-inch thickness.

Using a biscuit cutter and a knife, cut the dough into squares, triangles, and rectangles. Dip each into the butter to completely coat. Squeeze and press pieces into a nonstick Bundt pan until it is ⅔ full.

Cover with plastic wrap and place in a warm, draft-free place until the dough rises to the rim, about 1 hour. Bake until golden, about 35 minutes. If top browns too quickly, cover with aluminum foil and continue baking. To serve, unmold from Bundt pan and pull pieces off the loaf. *Makes 1 large loaf.*

◆ 110 ◆

୬ ୬

Äpfel im Schlafrock mit Himbeergeist
Apples Wrapped in Pastry with Raspberry Schnapps

"Apples dressed in sleeping coats" is the English translation. Wrapped in pastry and baked, these apples are served with a drop of *Himbeergeist*, a raspberry schnapps whose name means the soul of the raspberry. A small amount drizzled on top enhances the apple like nothing we know. If you can't find *Himbeergeist*, use applejack instead. Some of our guests like to add a scoop of vanilla ice cream on the side.

4–5 cups flour

1 teaspoon salt

⅔ cup vanilla sugar (available in gourmet shops or see page 41)

⅔ cup blanched slivered almonds, finely chopped and toasted

2 teaspoons grated lemon rind

⅔ cup (1 stick plus 3 tablespoons) unsalted butter, softened

2 large eggs, lightly beaten

2 tablespoons ice water

5 tablespoons sugar

⅓ cup seedless golden raisins

3 teaspoons cinnamon

1 tablespoon light rum

4 tablespoons orange marmalade

8 medium red Rome apples, cored and peeled

2 eggs, lightly beaten with 1 tablespoon water

1 cup Himbeergeist

Sift the flour, vanilla sugar, and salt together in a large bowl. Add the nuts and lemon rind. Using a pastry blender or 2 forks, cut in the butter until mixture is the texture of coarse crumbs. Add the eggs and ice water and stir until soft dough forms. Divide the dough into 2 equal portions and shape into 2 bricks. Wrap in plastic wrap and chill at least 3 hours.

Preheat the oven to 400° F. Line a baking sheet with parchment paper. Combine the sugar, raisins, cinnamon, rum, and marmalade in a small bowl and stir until well combined.

Roll one brick of dough to 14x14-inch square on a lightly floured surface. Cut into 4 7x7 squares. Roll trimmings into a ball and keep chilled.

Place an apple in the center of each square. Fill the hollow core with the sugar mixture. Bring the corners of dough up around the apple and mold to fit. Repeat with remaining dough until all the apples are filled and wrapped in pastry.

Roll out reserved trimmings to ⅛-inch thickness and, using small star- or leaf-shaped cookie cutters, cut the dough into shapes. Press a shape to the top of each apple. Roll a small piece of dough in your fingertips and press to the top to form the stem. Brush with egg wash and bake 10 minutes. Reduce heat to 350° F. and bake until crust is crisp and golden brown, about 35 minutes.

To serve, place a whole apple on a dessert plate and let your guests help themselves to the *Himbeergeist. Makes 8.*

ॐ ॐ

TOP RIGHT: *These apples are large and the almond-flavored dough is rich. Don't hesitate to serve half an apple for dessert.*
ABOVE RIGHT: *The dessert table is enhanced by the presence of one of Ruth's favorite antiques—a miniature stable, barnyard, and animals. Sam is so careful when he plays with it that we allow him his freedom with it for hours.*

Don't Worry, We'll Bring Dinner

Many of our friends feel the ideal gift is one of time. Time to take a walk together, chat, shop, visit, have lunch. Here's a great gift—a movable feast and time with friends! While we prepared this chowder feast for a sit-down meal, it could also be a home-delivered meal in a basket. The chowder and peppers stay warm for at least two hours in a double-walled pot. Even without the special pot, you can carry the meal in your own conventional pot and heat it up for your friends. As an extra gesture of thoughtfulness, pack napkins, candles, and ornaments for presents. Make it an event—a warming and welcomed gift.

Fourth Week of Advent

AN OPEN HOUSE

By this time, our super Silo staff members have been very busy Santa's helpers. They have mailed hundreds of packages all over the world, created unique gift baskets filled with food, pottery, and linens, tied endless bows, and made hundreds of pounds of gingerbread dough for the special holiday classes. It's time for a treat, a breather, a break.

The bare amaryllis bulbs that we started weeks ago are beginning to bloom—a sign that Christmas is very near. We set them out on a table right in the cooking school. We light four candles on the Advent wreath and host an open-house buffet of appetizer wreaths for the staff and our customers. The open house becomes the gentle boost we need to be able to work on through the season, feeling festive and passing on the joy. There surely will be more work to come—Christmas-tree hunting, gift wrapping, and last-minute preparations. But for now, we take the time to enjoy the day and each other.

The extra bread wreaths baked and frozen weeks ago become the main event at our party. This is an ideal buffet for casual entertaining. Everything from the smoky seafood to the hearty salad stays fresh and good-looking through the afternoon.

Smoked Seafood Wreath

Seafood Dressing

Salmon and Dill Wreath

Apple Salad Wreath

FAR LEFT: *In a room next to the Silo cooking school, the bread wreaths are ready to be prepared for the buffet.*

◆ 113 ◆

SMOKED SEAFOOD WREATH

1 13-inch Advent Bread Wreath (see recipe, page 16)
½ pound small smoked shrimp
½ pound smoked scallops
½ pound smoked mussels
½ pound smoked salmon, thinly sliced
2 bunches fresh parsley
1 bunch fresh chives
1—2 pounds cherry tomatoes
½ pound mushrooms, wiped clean
Seafood Dressing (recipe follows)

Place the bread wreath on a large serving platter. Skewer each shrimp with a sturdy, round
toothpick and stick one at a time into the wreath.
Do the same with each scallop and mussel.
Arrange randomly to please your eye.

Roll each slice of salmon to resemble a rosette;
fasten with a toothpick and stick into wreath.

Wash and trim the parsley; make small bouquets and tie with a chive spear. Use these bouquets to fill in the spaces between the seafood until
the wreath is completely covered (guests do not
eat the bread itself).

Place the cherry tomatoes and mushrooms in
serving bowls on the side. Place Seafood Dressing
in a bowl in the center of the wreath or on the
side. *Serves 20—30 with other wreaths.*

SEAFOOD DRESSING

2 cups crème fraîche, plain yogurt, or sour cream
4 ounces (½ cup) cream-style prepared horseradish
2 tablespoons chopped fresh chives

Combine all ingredients in a medium bowl.
Place bowl in a crock of chipped ice and serve.

೨ৎ

Better More Than Not Enough

When hosting an open house like this, we order
extra of what we feel will be the most popular
food on the table. In this case it was the smoked
seafood, cherry tomatoes, and mushrooms. We
ordered more than double what we needed and
placed the extras in bowls on the table.

Crisping the Bread Wreath

When defrosting a frozen bread wreath, allow it
to thaw in its wrapping. Then unwrap it and place
it in a 350° F. oven for 10 minutes to crisp the
crust and enliven the color.

ABOVE: *In the center of the seafood wreath, a green marble
crock holds ice that keeps the silver bowl of seafood dressing
well chilled.* RIGHT: *We planted amaryllis bulbs in metal sap
buckets. In bloom, they provide a table decoration of regal
stature. The butter tree at table's end was easily constructed
with softened butter and a pastry bag.*

SALMON AND DILL WREATH

1 13-inch Advent Bread Wreath (see recipe, page 16)
2 bunches fresh dill, trimmed, leaving 5 inches of stem
1 pound smoked salmon, sliced thin
1 bunch fresh chives, washed and patted dry
2 lemons, thinly sliced
2 bunches scallions, washed and patted dry
Seafood Dressing (see recipe, page 114)

Place the wreath on a large serving platter and cut it into 35 ½-inch slices, being careful to keep the slices in a circle.

Lay sprigs of dill over the wreath to cover.

Roll the salmon slices into loose bundles and tie in the center with a chive spear. Lay on top of the dill branches around the wreath. Place the lemon slices on the wreath to fill in between salmon bundles until wreath is covered. Do this to please your own eye. Garnish with scallions. Place a bowl of Seafood Dressing in the center of the wreath or to one side.

When your guests serve themselves from this wreath, encourage them to take a slice of the bread wreath as well. They'll make open-face salmon appetizers for themselves. *Serves 20–30 with other wreaths.*

❧ ❧

LEFT: *This delicious pre-sliced salmon and other smoked seafood came by mail from Duck Trap Farm in Belfast, Maine. Their fish is always beautifully smoked.*

APPLE SALAD WREATH

The salad is a combination of hearty salad ingredients and is arranged around the braided bread wreath, which holds the four candles symbolizing the four Sundays of Advent. You can choose any ingredients you like—watercress, radicchio, jícama—instead of the endive and lettuce. Just make sure you use hardy greens that can stay fresh-tasting and good-looking through an open-house afternoon.

4 medium red apples, cored and cut into 8 wedges each
Juice of 2 lemons
1 13-inch Advent Bread Wreath (see recipe, page 16)
8 heads Belgian endive, trimmed and quartered
*   lengthwise*
8 medium heads Bibb lettuce, washed and cut into quar-
*   ters, leaving core intact*
10 mushrooms, wiped clean and quartered
Apple Butter Horseradish Dressing (recipe follows)

Sprinkle the apples with the lemon juice, tossing to coat well. Set aside.

Place the wreath in the center of a round serving platter larger than the wreath (26–30 inches in diameter). Pizza pans are the perfect size. Slice wreath into 35 ½-inch slices, being careful to keep the slices in a circle. Place a circle of endive quarters around the outer edge of the platter. You will have to leave space between the endive slices to go all the way around the circle. Fill in the spaces with an overlapping circle of lettuce leaves closer to the wreath, then a circle of apples, then mushrooms closest to the wreath. Serve Apple Butter Horseradish Dressing in a bowl or crock fitted in the center of the wreath. *Serves 20–30 with other wreaths.*

᷐᷐ ᷐

ABOVE: *All four candles on our bread wreath announce the fourth Sunday of Advent. The bread wreath is at the center of our Apple Salad, which is easy to eat with the fingers.*

◆**117**◆

APPLE BUTTER HORSERADISH DRESSING

2 cups crème fraîche, plain yogurt, or sour cream
12 ounces apple butter or applesauce
4 ounces (½ cup) cream-style prepared horseradish
2 cups golden raisins
2 tablespoons chopped fresh chives

Combine the crème fraîche, apple butter, horseradish, and raisins in a medium bowl. Sprinkle with chives and place in center of wreath or on the side.

᷐᷐ ᷐

TEENS' SOUP AND LAMINGTONS PARTY

⁂

This is a wonderful young people's party. Parents can help prepare it, then leave the kids to have a good time on their own. In fact, any group of casual friends would enjoy this party. The food is simple—soup served with large bread branches (great for dunking), salad, punch, and Lamingtons for dessert.

A traditional sweet in Australia, Lamingtons were introduced to us by our Australian daughter-in-law, Sandra. We found them irresistible! They are small squares of pound cake dipped in chocolate then coated with coconut.

No one leaves the party until they've eaten their fill of everything and made a sackful of Lamingtons to take home as Christmas presents.

Hot Potato Turnip Soup

Bread Branches

Steamed Red Radish Salad

Ice Ring Punch

Lamingtons

⚬119⚬

FAR LEFT: *A low rough wood table in front of the Main House tree is the setting for this relaxed party.*

LEFT: *We saved pint-size vegetable and fruit baskets from years past especially for occasions such as this one—packing up Lamingtons for guests to take away.*

HOT POTATO TURNIP SOUP

We are surprised how much young people are aware of good-for-you food—how often they teach their parents about the latest in nutrition. Our teenage grandchildren are conscientious about choosing healthful food. They loved this soup!

BEEF STOCK

1 tablespoon vegetable oil

6–8 beef marrow bones, each 3–3½ inches thick

1 pound beef chuck, cut into 1½-inch cubes

2 medium onions, peeled and cut in half

1 teaspoon salt

1 teaspoon freshly ground pepper

2 medium carrots, scrubbed

2 stalks celery, with leaves

5 quarts warm water

4 bay leaves

6 peppercorns

2 large onions, peeled and coarsely chopped (about 2 cups)

1 pound turnips (about 3 medium), peeled and sliced

2 pounds potatoes (about 6 medium), peeled and sliced

3 sprigs fresh marjoram or 1 tablespoon dried marjoram

12–16 mini-frankfurters, or regular-sized frankfurters cut into thirds

Sprigs of fresh parsley for garnish

To make the stock, heat the oil in a large heavy stockpot. Add the bones and cook, turning with tongs, until brown. They will spatter and hiss, so be careful. Add the meats and continue cooking until brown.

Add the onion, salt, pepper, carrots, and celery and continue cooking until the onions are a deep golden color. Be careful not to burn. Add the water, bay leaves, and peppercorns and heat to boiling. Reduce heat and simmer, uncovered, 1 hour. Cover and continue simmering ½ hour. Remove from heat and let cool. Strain and discard solids. Pour into a glass bowl or container and refrigerate. This can be done the day before making the soup.

Skim off the white fat from the surface of the refrigerated stock and place 3 tablespoons of the fat in a large stockpot. Heat over medium-high heat. Add the onions and cook until transparent, about 5 minutes. Add the turnips and cook, turning carefully, for 5 minutes. Add the potatoes, marjoram, and stock. Heat to boiling; reduce heat and simmer until potatoes and turnips are cooked to taste, about 15 minutes. (We like the potatoes falling apart and the turnips a little firm.) Add the mini-franks. Remove from heat and allow franks to heat through. Ladle generous amounts into bowls and garnish with parsley. *Serves 6–10.*

BREAD BRANCHES

Encourage your teens to dunk these hearty "baguettes" into the soup.

1 packet (¼ ounce) active dry yeast

1¼ cups cold water

1 tablespoon sugar

2 tablespoons vegetable oil

4 cups flour

1 egg, well beaten

1 ounce (about 2 tablespoons) sesame seeds

¼ cup kosher salt (optional)

Dissolve the yeast in 2 tablespoons of the cold water in a large mixing bowl. Add the sugar, oil, and 3 cups of the flour and stir until a soft dough forms. Turn out onto a lightly floured surface and knead, adding more flour as needed, until the dough is smooth and elastic. Shape into a ball, cover with a clean damp towel, and let rest 30 minutes. Cut the dough into 24 portions and shape each into a ball about the size of a golf ball. Cover and let rest another 10 minutes.

Preheat the oven to 350° F. Line 2 15½x10½-inch baking sheets with parchment paper. Using your hands, roll each ball on a lightly floured surface to form a loaf 6 inches long; place on baking sheet. Brush each loaf with egg and sprinkle with seeds. Sprinkle with salt, if desired. Bake until golden and crisp, about 15 minutes. *Makes 24.*

❦ ❧

Mini-Franks Plus

Buy extra mini-franks and serve them hot in a large bowl on the buffet. Keep a bowl of ketchup on the side. This will make any teen feel comfortable. They can spear a frank with a sturdy toothpick and dip it in the ketchup.

Holiday time isn't necessarily the time to demand that kids eat sophisticated foods. Letting them be comfortable might be the best way to enjoy the season. Save new food adventures for springtime.

FAR LEFT: *The acorn tureen and matching bowls keep soup hot and draw admiring glances. When not in use, they are an eye-catching delight on mantel or shelf.*

LEFT: *Since this soup is so dunk-worthy, we make extra Bread Branches, tying them in bundles with steamed scallions. The Steamed Red Radish Salad is served in a striped squash bowl.*

STEAMED RED RADISH SALAD

4 bunches red radishes (about 30), trimmed, cleaned,
  and soaked in water overnight
½ cup walnut or vegetable oil
½ cup tarragon vinegar
1 tablespoon sugar
1 teaspoon salt
½ teaspoon freshly ground pepper
1 teaspoon caraway seeds

Drain the radishes and pat dry. Fit a food processor with the julienne blade; push the radishes through until you have thin strips. Heat the oil in a medium saucepan over medium heat. Add the radishes and stir well. Stir in the vinegar, sugar, salt, pepper, and caraway seeds. Cover the pot and reduce heat to low. Cook 5 minutes. Drain most of the cooking juices, leaving only enough so that mixture is moist.

Serve hot or at room temperature in a large bowl. *Serves 6–10.*

❧ ❧

Packing Up

To make packages for the Lamingtons, our granddaughter, Kythera, decorated brown paper bags with stencils. Your guests may also want to decorate their own bags. Have materials ready for them—small lunch bags, rubber stamps, felt-tip markers, paint, crayons, stickers, gold seals.

ABOVE RIGHT: *As the ice ring melts, it adds flavor to the punch, letting the individual citrus slices break free and float.*

ICE RING PUNCH

10 cups distilled water
3 limes, thinly sliced
3 lemons, thinly sliced
3–4 quarts cranberry juice

Fill a 10-inch ring mold with half the water and half the sliced fruit. Place in the freezer until set, about 3 hours. Add the remaining water and fruit and return to the freezer for 8 hours, or overnight. To unmold and serve, let the ice ring stand at room temperature 15 minutes.

Meanwhile, fill a punch bowl with the cranberry juice. Dip the ice ring mold into a basin of warm water. Invert and place the ring in a punch bowl. *Serves 6–10.*

❧ ❧

LAMINGTONS

Have plenty of these sweet treats made ahead of time, so that everyone can see what they look like and taste like. To make their own to take home, teens need a fondue pot or chafing dish, several fondue forks, and an assembly-line organization of ingredients. Young people get into it right away.

1 cup unsweetened cocoa powder
1 pound confectioners' sugar
1 tablespoon cornstarch
4 cups cold water
2 frozen pound cakes, 10¾ ounces each, thawed
24 ounces shredded sweetened coconut

Sift the cocoa, sugar, and cornstarch into a saucepan. Add ½ cup of the water and stir to make a paste. Add remaining water. Heat slowly, stirring constantly, for 15 minutes, until slightly thick.

Cut the cake into 1½-inch cubes. Place a cup of coconut in a small brown paper bag. Using a fondue fork or skewer, immerse a cake cube in the chocolate. Be quick but also make sure the cube is totally coated. Drop the cube into the coconut bag and close the bag tightly. Lightly shake the bag until the cube is coated with coconut. Place the Lamington on a tray sprinkled with coconut and allow to dry for 15–20 minutes. Repeat until all cubes are coated. *Makes 16–20.*

❧ ❧

ABOVE: *A large tray under the hot chocolate is for security. All the ingredients are ready, and the kids will make and eat their fill before bagging some to take home.*

CUT A TREE—GIVE A TREE—PLANT A TREE

❧ ❧

In the early days of our marriage, we lived in New York City. Skitch was musical director for NBC-TV and appeared with his orchestra on "The Tonight Show." Like everyone else in our neighborhood, we bought our Christmas tree from the local tree merchant who set up his seasonal stand on the sidewalk. But sometimes we were able to bring one big lovely tree as well as several small ones back from Sugarbush, Vermont, where we took winter ski weekends. We'd tie them all to the roof of the car.

In those days, a fresh little Christmas tree, bare or sparsely decorated, was a wonderful present to give somebody who lived in the city. During the holidays, we would often bring a small tree to a party as a gift for the host.

Now we live with hundreds—thousands—of Christmas trees on our farm. Some we planted when we moved here twenty-five years ago to create the thick woods we love around the farm. Over the

FAR LEFT: *From our grove of Christmas trees, young Daren Daniels found and chose his family's tree. His dad, Jack, cuts it down.*

ABOVE: *Skitch at work on "The Tonight Show" set at 30 Rockefeller Plaza.*

LEFT: *Hans helps drag our tree home to the 1836 Barn. It was a long day—we cut trees for the Main House and the 1836 House too.*

years, we planted six thousand more little Christmas trees. After seven years, they became large enough to start harvesting. The Northville Fire Department, our local volunteer brigade, cuts and sells them in the parking lot of the firehouse down the road to raise funds. All the Hendersons, friends of the family, and the Silo staff go tree hunting.

It's one of our big pleasures—going out together to select and cut the trees that will come in for Christmas. There'll be one for the 1836 Barn, one for the 1836 House, one for the Main House, and

TOP: *Each year, Doug and Drew Doerwald, Gary Lord, and Richard Hill come with a crane, flatbed truck, and winch to hoist the great tree into the Silo Gallery. It's always a big tree and a big event.* ABOVE: *The tree that went into the Silo Gallery in 1992 was one of our best-loved from the farm. It grew for twenty years next to the Main House. About five feet tall when we planted it, it was twenty-five feet high and consuming the house when we had to cut it down.* RIGHT: *Orrin Jones, a tree expert, helps us maintain the trees in our Christmas-tree grove.*

one for the cottage. A few days before Christmas, we all head down the hill. This year, young Daren Daniels and his dad, Jack, joined all of us on the tree expedition. It was Daren's first. What a dauntless hunter he was! He ran from tree to tree, looking at each carefully. His mother had told him to make sure he found one he really liked. Finally, he pointed to the perfect one—tall, thick, and full.

In the Northville Fire Department parking lot, it's an active scene as new trees arrive and families pick and choose and bargain. Ruth loves to visit; it reminds her of the years when her great-uncle Edwin and three of his sons would come to Plauen, Germany, her hometown, with loads and loads of Christmas trees to sell. She loved to watch Uncle Edwin and the boys set up right on the corner near her house in town. Her parents let her spend the day with them selling trees. To keep warm, they brought a black coal-fired stove and a big iron pot in which potatoes would bake all afternoon and evening. When they got hungry, they tossed a potato to one another until it cooled a bit. Ruth had a great time staying out with them while her mother kept a large one-pot meal warm on the stove at home. They would come in one at a time, bringing the strong smell of pines with them. They'd warm up with a good meal, then go back out to the cold and trees.

When we cut a very large tree, like the twenty-foot one we bring into the Silo Gallery, some people are horrified. How can you do such a thing, they ask. The fact is that we planted so many when we moved here that some now grow too close to one another and too close to buildings. We have to cut those to save others.

In spring or early fall, we plant new trees to take the place of those we've cut from our Christmas-tree forests. There will be new trees planted again this year in the names of our grandchildren, Keiran, Kythera, Will, and Sam.

It seems we're still giving trees.

TOP: *Rex, our Lakeland terrier, is a fearless winter companion. He cavorts in the snow and loves to be included in all outdoor activities.* ABOVE: *It's a long haul from the Christmas-tree grove to the 1836 Barn. Keiran, with Isabelle and Rex, supervises.*

RIBS, SAUSAGE, AND BEANS BUFFET

Hearty bowls of meaty ribs and beans welcome the Christmas-tree choosers, cutters, haulers, tag-alongers, and watchers. We set the buffet so that it would be surrounded by the red-red of the poinsettias, many of which had been arriving as presents from friends all week. We added to them until we had enough to set a wall ablaze with color.

The woodsmen ate ravenously.

FAR LEFT: *Under a Grandma Moses harvest scene, the Christmas-tree-hunters' buffet has been keeping warm in our favorite Swiss pots by Kuhn Rikon. Because of their double-wall design, the food stays warm; because of their beauty, they fit on any elegant or rustic buffet.*

LEFT: *The sun streaming through the barn windows makes the poinsettias even more vivid.*

❖ 129 ❖

RIBS, SAUSAGES, BEANS

24 ounces Silo Thirteen Bean Mix or any mixture of
    dried beans

2 quarts water

6–8 spareribs (about 2 pounds)

½ teaspoon salt

¼ teaspoon freshly ground pepper

½ teaspoon dried marjoram

2 teaspoons vegetable oil

1 large onion, peeled and coarsely chopped

2 bay leaves

6 peppercorns

2 cups beef or chicken stock (optional)

8 links hot Italian sausage, smoked sausage, or kielbasa

4 ounces red-pepper sauce (optional)

Balsamic vinegar

1 large red onion, roughly chopped

1 red bell pepper, seeded and roughly chopped

Place the beans in a large pot or bowl and
cover with the water. Soak at least 5 hours or
overnight.

Rub the ribs with salt, pepper, and marjoram
and allow to sit at room temperature 1 hour.

Heat 1 teaspoon of the oil in a large soup pot
over medium-high heat until hot but not smoking.
Add the ribs and cook until brown on all sides,
about 5 minutes. Transfer to a plate. Reduce heat
and add the onions. Cook, stirring frequently, 5
minutes. Add the beans with the soaking water and
the ribs. Heat to boiling; add bay leaves and peppercorns. Reduce heat and simmer, covered, until
the beans are tender, about 1 hour. Add the beef or
chicken broth if the mixture becomes too thick.

Meanwhile, heat the remaining oil in a large
skillet over medium-high heat until hot but not
smoking. Add the sausage and cook, turning often,
until brown, about 8 minutes. Transfer with a slotted spoon to a plate. When cooled slightly, cut into
½-inch round slices.

Add the sausage and red-pepper sauce to the
beans and ribs. Simmer 5 minutes.

To serve, ladle into warm bowls. Sprinkle with
vinegar, onions, and bell peppers. *Serves 6–8.*

ABOVE: *Here is a meal in a basket—ready to eat, piping
hot—that is especially welcome at Hans and Sandra's.*

RIGHT: *A sprig of marjoram adds color and bouquet to the
hearty meal.*

WRAPPING THE GIFTS

❧ ❧

There's a room in the 1836 Barn—Heidi's old bedroom—that becomes storage for glass and tin containers, baskets, bags of all sizes, string, ribbon, hay rope, remnants of old wallpaper, burlap, saved scraps of bright material, green felt, and stacks of newspapers to be used for wrapping presents.

At the beginning of Advent, we start saving newspaper. We keep sections with certain people in mind. We'll wrap a book about baseball for a fan in the Sunday sports section of *The New York Times*. Hans and friends who love computers might get a gift wrapped in the computer ads. Kythera—fashion. Keiran—movies! A journalist we know might get something wrapped in appropriate headlines; a young friend, perhaps the Sunday funnies. On the outside of each package, Ruth draws a tree with green marker. We often tie it with simple string or hay rope. Sometimes the wrapping itself is a present. Heidi was thrilled to receive a gift from us wrapped in a piece of the wallpaper from the room she grew up in. None of us remember the present, but we all remember her excited reaction to the paper.

We try to package and wrap with materials that have had a previous life and could have a life again after presents. Gifts for the pantry are all in reusable containers, simply adorned with bright material or a swatch of burlap tied over the top. Sometimes a dried flower, pine cone, or shining bell comes attached. Small and large baskets are perfect for an assortment of pantry presents, cookies wrapped in cellophane, stuffed toys, and children's books.

Small shopping bags, too, have a great afterlife!

OPPOSITE, TOP RIGHT: *All during Advent, we light up the farm with tiny white lights on fences, posts, and branches. The first indoor lights come from the tree we trim first, in the 1836 House. At night it's the one we can see from the path between the barn and the Silo, and it puts us in the mood to huddle in and wrap presents.*

◆ 133 ◆

OPPOSITE, TOP LEFT: *No gift tags are necessary with these packages. Hans and Heidi recognize the wallpaper from their childhood rooms. Skitch easily spots Daly's black and white.*

OPPOSITE, BOTTOM LEFT: *We use natural baskets, burlap, and felt for wrapping gifts. The gift tags are thin wood animal ornaments.*

OPPOSITE, BOTTOM RIGHT: *A basket full of pantry gifts is decorated with branches from our mini-orange tree. A metal cow planter holds paperwhite bulbs.*

Christmas Eve Dinner and Presents

❧ ❧

When Ruth was a little girl, she truly believed she heard the footsteps of Santa leaving the dining room on Christmas Eve. That's where her parents had set up the tree and closed the doors. She wasn't allowed into the room until after Santa had been there.

Meanwhile, her father, Kurt, took hours to decorate the tree, complete with real candles held to each branch with silver clips. *Am Heiligen Abend*—on December 24 at 6:00 p.m.—the family sat together in anticipation. Ruth could only look at the closed doors to the dining room and feel the growing excitement. Would Santa come? She played the piano and performed, singing two Christmas songs—"O Tannenbaum" and "Stille Nacht, Heilige Nacht"—and it was always during the last lyrics, "Sleep in heavenly peace," that she was sure she heard Santa's boots on the floor in the dining room. He was there!

Finally, when they were sure Santa had left, her parents opened the doors. The tree was aglow with candlelight. The presents sparkled, too, piled under the tree, and the night of excitement, food, and laughter had begun.

The particular joy of Christmas Eve hit home for Skitch much later in life. After World War II, he had his own dance band and agreed to play two afternoon shows on Christmas Eve for the inmates at Michigan State Penitentiary. The men had contributed a few cents a day from their pay at their prison jobs to hire Skitch. He bused the band, six show girls, two singers, a juggler, and an animal

Einsiedel Goulash

Christmas Roots

Puffed Potatoes

Christmas-Tree Pasta and Sauce for Toddlers

Persimmon Pudding with Poached Pears

◆135◆

FAR LEFT: Gesegnete Mahlzeit—guten Appetit—Boom! *This blessing was first said in German by Ruth's mother, who devised it so that those who speak only English can hold hands and join in on the final* Boom! *Skitch, Will, Ruth, Peter Dubos, Eileen FitzGerald, June Freemanzon, Hans, Sandra, Keiran, Kythera (not visible in the picture), Heidi, and Sam all say the blessing. A blessed meal—A good appetite—Boom!*

RIGHT: *We planted this tree near the 1836 Barn, and we can see it when we look out toward the horse pasture.*
BELOW: *An iron hat tree holds needlepoint stockings embroidered with names. There's always a piece of coal in the toe of each sock, and whatever we know the person likes—imported chocolate, marzipan, a photo in a tiny frame, popcorn, personal small gifts of perfume, pens, crayons for the kids, tiny toys—all the small and wonderful things of Christmas.*
FAR RIGHT: *The tree sits on top of our round oak table. Gifts are piled on the table and in the open drawers. The large ones underneath provide easy access for the little ones. Santa watches from the old English pantry cabinet.*

act up to the grim prison. Although no one said anything, he knew the performers all had the same sinking hearts. None of them had ever played for an audience of inmates—who could know what to expect!

But what an audience they were! For one thing, it was a treat to play to a packed auditorium of the uninebriated. They were alive with applause, cheers, whistles, and laughter. They loved the band, and the band loved them. It was tough to leave that night. One group was heading out to freedom, the other back to their cells. Skitch and the band gave the inmates a Christmas they'd remember for a long time, and they gave Skitch a very special Christmas Eve memory that he'll have forever.

Nowadays, we carry on many of Ruth's family traditions. No children are allowed in the Great Room for two days before Christmas, while preparations for Santa are in progress. Skitch's Christmas concerts still keep him on the road during much of Advent. On Christmas Eve, though, Skitch makes it home, often arriving with just enough time to write gift tags and attach them to presents. He then lights the candles in the Great Room and the big celebration begins.

ABOVE: *Cranberry juice is served from a Mexican glass decanter with a mercury glass stopper. To decorate the table, we bring out some of our snow-globe music boxes. We use green-and-white dish towels for napkins.*

RIGHT: *The little ginger-bread-house place cards become gifts to take home.*

FAR RIGHT: *Music warms the hearts of us all and bridges the generation gap.*

With two toddlers in the family, the night before Christmas is really exciting. We plan an early dinner—5:00 p.m.—and set the table with unbreakables so no one has to worry about fast-flying curious little hands. Red and white enamelware on silver chargers are set on durable green felt, which becomes the tablecloth. There are snow globes and wooden toys for decoration, and at each place is an edible gingerbread house with a name on it, which can be carried home later (smaller versions of the ones on pages 91–95). Tall child-proof battery-powered tapers light the table and the windowsills.

A few minutes before dinner, Skitch pulls out the stops of the pipe organ in the loft above us and the Great Room reverberates with Christmas music. The excitement builds as we are surrounded by the smells of food and fire and the sight of the tree set high up on a table with presents piled under. We sit for the meal, but not for long. Dinner is warming; it is substantial but not fancy—nothing must compete with the tree and the anticipation of opening the presents. Often we leave the food in the wonderful heat-saving double-walled pots on the sideboard, where it stays warm for two hours. Whoever is too excited to eat before opening presents can always return.

EINSIEDEL GOULASH

1¼ cups flour

3 teaspoons dried marjoram

3 teaspoons paprika

½ teaspoon salt

¼ teaspoon freshly ground pepper

2 pounds lean beef, cut into 1-inch cubes

2 pounds pork, cut into 1-inch cubes

5 tablespoons canola oil

3 large onions, diced (about 3½ cups)

2 cups beef broth

2 pounds veal, cut into 1-inch cubes

5 ounces prosciutto, diced

16 ounces mushrooms, wiped clean and cut in half

10 cornichons, thinly sliced

1 cup buttermilk

Combine 1 cup of the flour with the marjoram, paprika, salt, and pepper in a medium shallow bowl. Add the beef and pork and toss to coat well.

Heat the oil in a large saucepan or soup pot. Add the beef and pork a few pieces at a time and cook until medium-brown on all sides. Using a slotted spoon, transfer the meat to a plate. Add the onions to the pot and cook until soft, about 8 minutes. Return the browned meat to the pot. Add the broth and heat to boiling; reduce heat and simmer 45 minutes. Add the veal, prosciutto, and mushrooms; continue simmering another 30 minutes. Add the cornichons and simmer 10 minutes.

Combine the remaining flour, buttermilk, and ¼ cup hot goulash broth in a small bowl. Stir until well blended. Slowly add the buttermilk mixture to the simmering goulash and stir well. Continue simmering 5 minutes. *Serves 12.*

❧ ❧

CHRISTMAS ROOTS

8 medium carrots, peeled and sliced

8 parsnips, peeled and sliced

1 large turnip, peeled and sliced

1½ cups chicken broth

1 tablespoon light brown sugar

Salt and freshly ground pepper to taste

½ cup warm milk or half-and-half (optional)

½ cup chopped fresh parsley

Place the vegetables in a medium saucepan. Add the chicken broth and cook over medium heat until vegetables are tender, about 15 minutes. Mash with a potato masher in the pot until almost smooth. Stir in sugar and salt and pepper. Add milk if desired. Serve sprinkled with parsley. *Serves 12.*

❧ ❧

PUFFED POTATOES

If you don't have a convection oven, there are fans now available that turn a regular oven into a convection oven.

1½ pounds sweet potatoes (about 3 medium), scrubbed and cut into ⅛-inch-thick slices

2 pounds baking potatoes (about 3 large), scrubbed and cut into ⅛-inch-thick slices

1 pound red potatoes (about 3 medium), scrubbed and cut into ⅛-inch-thick slices

Preheat a convection oven to 350° F. Place separated potato slices on a rack on a baking sheet. Bake until puffy and brown, about 30 minutes. *Serves 12.*

❧ ❧

CHRISTMAS-TREE PASTA AND SAUCE FOR TODDLERS

All specialty food stores offer pasta in different shapes and colors. The Christmas-tree shape must have been designed with small children in mind. Will and Sam love it! Any pasta with a simple tomato sauce is the perfect dish for those with finicky and undeveloped taste buds. A good pantry stock of canned tomatoes and sauce is essential for quick and pleasing pasta meals for kids and adults. Be sure to keep your own trusted brands on hand.

1 35-ounce can whole tomatoes

½ cup tomato paste

1 10-ounce package frozen peas

1 pound tree-shaped pasta

Olive oil

Combine the whole tomatoes and tomato paste in a large saucepan. (If you like the sauce smooth, puree the tomatoes. We prefer a chunkier sauce.) Heat to boiling; reduce heat and simmer 10 minutes. Add the peas and simmer 5 minutes longer.

Meanwhile, cook the pasta in boiling salted water until tender. Drain. Drizzle with olive oil and place in a serving bowl, or, as we did, in a Christmas-tree mold. Pass the sauce on the side.

৽ৄ ঽ

ABOVE: *We serve the pasta in a large Christmas-tree mold surrounded by fresh evergreen branches. Nearby is a carved figure of Skitch as cook, wielding a spoon instead of a baton.*

PERSIMMON PUDDING WITH POACHED PEARS

We ordered pomegranates from the market and got persimmons by mistake. When life hands you persimmons, make persimmon pudding!

10 medium-large persimmons
4 eggs
1¼ cups sugar
2 cups flour
1½ teaspoons baking powder
1½ teaspoons baking soda
½ teaspoon salt
1½ cups milk
1 cup half-and-half
2½ teaspoons cinnamon
1½ teaspoons ground ginger
½ teaspoon freshly grated nutmeg
1 cup golden raisins soaked in water or rum

TOPPING

3 ripe Red Bartlett pears, poached and thinly sliced, 1 cup blanched slivered almonds, 1 cup chopped roasted chestnuts, 1 cup fresh cranberries

Preheat the oven to 350° F. Lightly grease a 9x12-inch, 3-quart baking dish and set aside.

Cut the persimmons in half and scrape out the flesh. Discard skin. Place flesh in the container of a food processor or blender and process until smooth.

Beat the eggs in a large bowl. Add the persimmon pulp and beat well. Add all remaining ingredients and stir until well blended. Pour into the prepared dish. Bake until set, about 1 hour. Allow to cool slightly. Before serving, top as desired. *Serves 12.*

LEFT: *Our pudding was made two days ahead. Just before serving, we chose to top it simply with poached pears and then fill the center with raspberry syrup.*

RIGHT: *Our house in New York was a lively place to celebrate Christmas. With cathedral ceilings, it would fill up with the fragrance and spirit of the holidays.*

Those Presents! Then and Now

It seems that it's the small gifts that give our family the most pleasure. A small carving to add to a collection, a toy, a silver frame with a picture of the kids. A poem or a word on a card can make Christmas Eve memorable. Once, when Hans and Heidi were teenagers, we found two small Victorian leather-bound photo albums at a flea market. Each page contained room for just one oval photo. We removed the existing pictures and replaced them with pictures from Hans and Heidi's albums, making a small keepsake for each. We were astounded to see that those albums were their favorite gifts.

Ruth still uses the small manicure set Hans gave her when he was fifteen.

Recently we've begun to recycle gifts. The Franklin Mint collector's coins that Hans never really liked as a boy was a big hit when he opened it this Christmas.

Keiran loved his camera, complete with lenses and accessories, recycled from Ruth, who never really did learn to use it. Keiran never puts it down.

One Christmas Kythera received a big box of beautiful fabrics, buttons, sequins, garlands, and scarves. Before the night was through, she had fashioned herself a beautiful dress with pins. The following year, we gave her a sewing machine.

Last year, Will and Sam were delighted with their basket filled with wooden blocks of all shapes and colors, and wooden trucks and trains their mother and their uncle Hans played with as children. They especially loved Freddy, Heidi's beloved stuffed horse, which comes alive when a young rider mounts it—it's not a rocking horse, but one that moves and bounces forward. It was "the" kid's gift in 1966.

Christmas Day

As a child, Ruth got up very early Christmas morning, while everyone else slept. It was her private time to play with the toys of Christmas. Most often, she played first and longest with the toys that reappeared under the tree year after year. By far the most exciting toy that returned each Christmas was Ruth's own store. This was a child-size counter one could stand behind, with shelves filled with jars of real mini-candies, real rice and small noodles, and baskets of small marzipan fruits and potatoes. There was a scale with miniature brass weights to weigh it all out and little brown bags to put it all in. A register rang when the keys were pressed and wooden money sat in the change drawer. It's such a vivid memory—anyone can see it's no surprise that Ruth became a shopkeeper in later life.

Later on Christmas morning, Ruth tore herself away from her presents and toys and got into the car with her mother and father and her mother's parents, Grandma (Omi) and Grandpa (Opi) List, for the hour-long drive to her Omi and Opi Einsiedel's home in nearby Greiz. For Ruth, the best part of the trip was arriving and being able to see her Opi Einsiedel's rabbits. Everybody enjoyed an ample feast of Christmas Day goose.

These days, Ruth is still the first one up on Christmas morning. When radio music plays softly through the barn, it's the first sign that Skitch is awake. After breakfast, Skitch will take both Sam and Will on a special outdoor trip to wish Merry Christmas to all our farm friends. They'll carry a basket full of presents for all the animals.

OPPOSITE: *We cherish these pictures, since all Ruth's family albums were destroyed in the Second World War. Her family's customs and traditions are part of our holiday celebrations today.* TOP LEFT: *Marie and Arno List, Ruth's maternal grandparents.* TOP RIGHT: *Kurt and Hildegard Einsiedel, Ruth's parents. They loved to visit our farm and called it an oasis.* MIDDLE RIGHT: *Ruth and Omi Einsiedel. She was always marinating meat, canning fruits and vegetables, or baking—much to Ruth's delight.* BOTTOM RIGHT: *Marie and Richard Einsiedel, Ruth's paternal grandparents. Their house was surrounded by flowers, berries, fruit trees, and an immense vegetable garden. The fragrance of it all is unforgettable.* BOTTOM LEFT: *Omi List, matriarch, entrepreneur, tireless caregiver, and independent woman— all four feet three inches of her!*

◆145◆

ANIMAL PRESENTS ON
CHRISTMAS DAY

᪐

Our dogs, Rex, Sheba, and Isabelle, our numerous cats, and our horses, Jupiter and Salome, are constant and comforting presences in our lives. We make sure they get an edible present early on Christmas morning.

DOG AND CAT BISCUITS

We make these biscuits a few weeks before Christmas. Packed in a gift jar, they make great presents for animal lovers and for the animals they love.

6 teaspoons soft margarine, lard, or bacon fat
1 teaspoon brown sugar
1 egg, lightly beaten
½ cup powdered milk
½ cup chicken broth
1 cup flour
1 cup whole-wheat flour
½ cup wheat germ
½ teaspoon salt
½ cup catnip (for cats)

FAR LEFT, CLOCKWISE FROM TOP RIGHT: *Sheba squints into the bright white expanse; Jupiter and Salome forage in the pasture—they love to lick up the new-fallen snow; Isabelle sits in the middle of the road after a big snowfall. These Silo cats live in the old milk house, near enough to the cooking school for them to be treated with leftovers.*

Preheat the oven to 325° F. Lightly grease a cookie sheet.

Cream the margarine and sugar together in the bowl of an electric mixer until light. Beat in the egg, powdered milk, and broth.

Attach the dough hook and gradually add the flours, wheat germ, and salt, and knead until a soft dough forms. Shape into a ball; cover and let rest 30 minutes. Roll out on a lightly floured surface to ¼-inch thickness. If making cat biscuits, sprinkle liberally with catnip and pat with fingertips into dough.

Using a 3-inch fish- or bone-shaped cookie cutter, cut out biscuits and place on prepared cookie sheet. Bake until lightly brown and crisp, about 30 minutes. Cool on a rack. Pack in airtight containers. *Makes about 3 dozen.*

JUNIE'S CHRISTMAS MIDDAY MEAL

Since there are so many of us living so close to one another at Hunt Hill Farm, cooking and entertaining are often shared. Christmas Eve is at our house, while the Christmas Day meal is cooked and served by our dear friend June Freemanzon in Hunt Hill Cottage. We love hearty Italian country food but rarely prepare it for ourselves. So it's a pleasure when our neighbor cooks her favorite cuisine.

What a treat to wake up Christmas morning, enjoy the early hours with family and our animal friends, and then later stroll over to Hunt Hill Cottage for this robust midday meal. Outside the cottage, a bare tree decorated with colorful birds, handcrafted by Canadian Sioux Indians, welcomes us. We carry a few presents that we saved unopened from the night before. It feels like a small vacation.

Antipasto

Parmesan-Stuffed Mushrooms

Chicken Scarpariello

Penne Pomodoro

Watercress Tomato Salad

Cottage Crème de la Crème

◆ **149** ◆

FAR LEFT: *Many years ago in Du Quoin, Illinois, we found these hand-beaded ornaments for sale at the state fair. We've never seen anything like them again, but we're always on the lookout.*

LEFT: *Rex is the only leash dog on the farm, because his interest in passing vehicles and horses is a little too intense. The only time he can run free is on his morning walk with Ruth up the mountain.*

PARMESAN-STUFFED MUSHROOMS

24 large, firm, white mushrooms, wiped clean
1 medium onion, peeled and finely chopped
1 stalk celery, trimmed, finely chopped
2 tablespoons olive oil
6 tablespoons freshly grated Parmesan cheese
6 tablespoons toasted breadcrumbs

Preheat oven to 350° F. Lightly oil a baking sheet.

Remove the stems from the mushrooms and chop fine. Reserve the mushroom caps. Combine the chopped stems, onion, and celery in a small bowl.

Heat the oil in a medium skillet over medium heat until hot. Add the mushroom mixture and cook until lightly browned. Add 3 tablespoons of the cheese and the breadcrumbs. Stir until the mixture holds together. Allow to cool slightly, then spoon into mushroom caps. Place the stuffed mushrooms on prepared baking sheet and sprinkle evenly with remaining cheese. Bake until the mushrooms are just soft and tops are golden, about 8 minutes. Do not overcook. *Makes 24 mushrooms.*

⤚ ⤙

ANTIPASTO

The secret here is to have plenty and arrange it on a platter to please your own eye.

½ pound salami, thinly sliced
½ pound pepperoni, thinly sliced
½ pound prosciutto, thinly sliced
½ pound mozzarella cheese, thinly sliced
1 5-ounce jar black oil-cured olives, with pits
1 5-ounce jar green olives, with pits
1 14-ounce can artichoke hearts, drained and cut in half
1 12-ounce jar pimientos
1 2-ounce can anchovies
1 bunch fresh Italian parsley for garnish

Arrange all ingredients on a platter to suit your eye. Garnish with parsley. *Serves 10–12.*

⤚ ⤙

ABOVE LEFT: *The antipasto is set against Junie's favorite color combination of blue and white.*

CHICKEN SCARPARIELLO

2 chickens (about 3 pounds each), cut into small pieces
(leave legs whole)
¼ cup plus 1 tablespoon olive oil
¼ cup chopped fresh rosemary
¼ cup chopped fresh parsley
Salt and freshly ground pepper to taste
3 pounds sweet Italian sausage
4 cloves garlic, peeled and thinly sliced
4 red bell peppers, seeded, and quartered
2 green bell peppers, seeded, and quartered
1 red bell pepper, cut into thin round slices
1 bunch parsley for garnish

Rub chicken pieces with 1 tablespoon oil and sprinkle with rosemary, parsley, and salt and pepper. Let stand for 30 minutes.

Heat about ¾ cup water in a large skillet over medium-high heat. When simmering, add the sausage and steam, turning often, until water has evaporated, about 5 minutes. Prick the sausage with a fork and continue cooking, turning often, until browned on all sides, about 8 minutes. Remove from pan with a slotted spoon. Add ¼ cup water to pan juices and reserve for use in following penne recipe.

When sausages have cooled slightly, cut each into ½-inch slices. Set aside.

Preheat the oven to 350° F.

Heat the remaining oil in a large heavy skillet over medium-high heat. Add the garlic and sauté until lightly brown, then remove from pan with a slotted spoon. Add the chicken and cook in batches until brown on all sides, about 6 to 8 minutes. Transfer to a plate and set aside.

Cook the quartered peppers in boiling salted water for 2 minutes, then drain. Combine the pep-

pers, chicken, and sausage in a roaster or large casserole. Cover and bake 45 minutes.

To serve, place in a serving bowl or leave in the casserole. Arrange red pepper slices on top and add fresh parsley to garnish. *Serves 10–12.*

᧬᧭

ABOVE: *Junie serves buffet-style, right out of the pot. Christmas mums form the centerpiece.*

PENNE POMODORO

3 tablespoons olive oil

3 large onions, peeled and coarsely chopped

3 28-ounce cans Italian peeled tomatoes with basil

3 tablespoons chopped fresh parsley or 1 tablespoon dried
    parsley

3 tablespoons chopped fresh basil or 1 tablespoon dried
    basil

1 tablespoon finely chopped fennel leaves or 2 teaspoons
    dried fennel

1 tablespoon chopped oregano or 1 teaspoon dried
    oregano

Reserved pan juices from Chicken Scarpariello recipe
    (page 151)

3 pounds dried penne

Chopped fresh basil for garnish (optional)

Chopped fresh parsley for garnish (optional)

½ cup freshly grated Parmesan cheese for garnish

Heat the oil in a large heavy skillet or saucepan over medium-high heat. Add the onions and cook until lightly brown, about 6–8 minutes. Add the tomatoes and stir to crush. Heat to boiling; reduce heat and simmer 30 minutes. Add the parsley, basil, fennel, oregano, and reserved juices. Simmer 30 minutes longer.

Meanwhile, cook the penne in boiling salted water until tender. Drain and transfer to a large serving bowl. Add ½ the sauce and toss to coat well. Garnish with fresh basil or parsley. Serve extra sauce and Parmesan cheese on the side.

৯৯ ২৯

WATERCRESS TOMATO SALAD

3 bunches fresh watercress, trimmed, washed, and patted
    dry

½ cup olive oil

¼ cup red-wine vinegar

6 teaspoons dry mustard

Freshly ground pepper to taste

½ pound cherry tomatoes, sliced

Place the watercress in a serving bowl. Whisk the oil, vinegar, mustard, and pepper together in a small bowl. Pour over salad and toss. Line the inside rim of the bowl with the tomato slices. *Serves 10–12.*

৯৯ ২৯

Sharing the Holiday

More and more families and friends are sharing the work and joy of big holidays. There are pot-luck Thanksgivings and long holiday weekends shared by neighbors and friends. One family hosts Christmas Eve; someone else does Christmas Day. Yet another does afternoon dessert. Someone else does a New Year's buffet. The tight family unit is expanding to create extended family out of neighbors and friends. For us, this makes holidays even more memorable.

Cottage Crème de la Crème

This is a wonderful dessert that is assembled in a food processor and chilled. The recipe can also be made in a blender, if you prepare half of it at a time.

2 10-ounce packages frozen strawberries, thawed
1 10-ounce package (4 envelopes) unflavored gelatin
½ cup cold water or milk
½ cup sugar
4 eggs, lightly beaten
2 cups crushed ice
2 cups heavy cream
6 fresh strawberries, sliced

Lightly oil two 1½-quart soufflé dishes.

Drain 1 cup of juice from the frozen berries and heat in a small saucepan over medium heat until simmering. Pour the juice, gelatin, and water into the container of a food processor and process 40 seconds. Add the sugar and eggs; process 5 seconds. Add the berries; process 5 seconds. Add the ice and cream; process 20 seconds. Pour into prepared soufflé dishes and chill at least 3 hours.

Serve garnished with a fan of strawberry slices. *Serves 10.*

৯৯ ২৯

ABOVE RIGHT: *Dessert is served on a wooden Shaker tray, surrounded by gingerbread animals.*

RIGHT: *We visit the owl sculpture that lives on a metal branch near the tobacco barn and admire his winter coat.*

THE LEBKUCHEN DESSERT BUFFET

❧ ❧

After the midday meal at Junie's, there is a must-take walk with the grandchildren. We take treats from the table to the animals, who always seem to know we're coming and welcome us. Then we head for what's waiting in the 1836 House—another family tradition, the Lebkuchen dessert buffet. It's a mouthwatering collection of sweet cakes and cookies prepared by the bakery of E. Otto Schmidt in Nürnberg, Germany, a town famous for Lebkuchen. For years and years, Ruth's parents sent us a large ornate tin chest packed with a huge selection of the sweet cakes. Now, we order them for ourselves, friends, and colleagues.

Each sweet cake or cookie is itself a work of art. And each has its own name and design. *Elisen Lebkuchen*, said to be the best of them all, are made, according to tradition, with at least 25 percent nuts (usually almonds) and no more than 10 percent flour. Sometimes they are glazed and sometimes covered with chocolate. *Spekulatius* are spiced almond biscuits shaped in classic patterns. There are at least a dozen varieties in a large tin.

The tin chest itself becomes a collector's item, since no Christmas design is ever repeated. We keep ours from year to year. Each is put to good use, storing everything from old photographs to pasta.

FAR LEFT: *We use a large "slice" of the old maple tree, felled by the storm of 1992, for a giant tray. Seventeen and a half pounds of Lebkuchen (literally, "life cakes") come packed in a beautiful collector's tin.*

Zweiter Feiertag!

THE SECOND HOLIDAY

⤜⤛ ⤜

In Germany, as in England, the day after Christmas is a second holiday, celebrated with as much joy as Christmas Day. *Zweiter Feiertag* was also the day in Plauen, Ruth's hometown, when those with a wealth of gifts and food would share with those who had very little. It was a simple custom set up through churches and schools. In fact, all through the year, Ruth's mother quietly looked out for several big families that lived nearby. During school, Ruth often brought several children home with her for lunch. So, *Am Zweiten Feiertag*, there were sure to be lots of presents—toys, hats, scarves, mittens, candy, and cookies to be delivered to neighboring families. Then, later in the day, friends and relatives would get together for another feast.

Here on the farm, since Junie had treated the whole clan to a Christmas midday meal, we decided to extend our holiday together and invite her to a second holiday dinner. We cooked a goose, which would be the usual Christmas Day meal in Germany. This meal was just for grownups. Sam and Will were napping; Keiran and Kythera were submerged in their books and videos. We sat in the quiet of the 1836 House and lounged our way through this comforting feast.

Gänsebraten
ROAST GOOSE

Warm Pears and Chestnuts

Grüne Klösse
POTATO DUMPLINGS

Red Cabbage and Apples

Pistachio Ice Cream Tree
with Warm Red Currant
Sauce

Gelatin Dessert Trees

◆ 157 ◆

FAR LEFT: Gänsebraten *with Warm Pears and Chestnuts and Grüne Klösse formed Ruth's family's traditional Christmas meal. Bundles of sage and marjoram surround the goose.*

ABOVE: *The goose is carved on a large copper platter, and surrounded by pears and chestnuts.*

LEFT: *Dried artichokes, sprayed silver and fitted with candles, sit in a copper colander surrounded by natural pine cones, creating the centerpiece at our table.*

Gänsebraten
Roast Goose

Choose a firm, white goose. Ours was a frozen free-range bird. It took 2 days to thaw in the refrigerator, so plan that into your preparation time. We poached our goose before roasting to rid it of excess fat.

1 9–11-pound goose

STOCK
2 stalks celery, with leaves
2 onions, peeled and cut in half
2 medium carrots, scrubbed
2 bay leaves
6 black peppercorns
1 teaspoon salt
3 quarts water
1 teaspoon unsalted butter

6 large sprigs fresh sage or 2 teaspoons dried sage
6 large sprigs fresh marjoram or 2 teaspoons dried marjoram
1½ teaspoons salt
1½ teaspoons freshly ground pepper
12 medium shallots, peeled
2 carrots, scrubbed and trimmed
6 juniper berries
1 large baking potato, scrubbed
2 tablespoons unsalted butter
3 tablespoons flour

Wipe the goose with a clean, wet towel and remove the giblets from the cavity. Combine the giblets (except for the liver), celery, onions, carrots, bay leaves, peppercorns, and salt in a large stockpot. Add the water. Heat to boiling; reduce heat and simmer, uncovered, until reduced by ⅓, about 1½ hours. Remove the giblets with a slotted spoon. Cool giblets slightly and chop fine. Reserve. Strain the stock and keep warm.

Heat the butter in a small skillet. Add the reserved liver and cook until brown on all sides. Remove with a slotted spoon. Cool slightly and chop fine. Set aside.

Ladle ¼ cup of simmering giblet stock into a small bowl. Add sage and marjoram and steep 3 minutes. Remove the herbs with a small sieve and return broth to saucepan. Set the herbs aside to cool.

Wipe the cavity of the goose with a clean, wet towel. Place the goose in a large roasting pan or a pot large enough to allow it to lie breast up. Rub the cavity with salt and pepper. Insert the steeped and reserved herbs, shallots, carrots, and juniper berries.

Place the potato in the opening of the cavity; it will act as a stopper and save you the trouble of trussing.

Pour enough warm water over the goose to come halfway up the sides of the bird. Heat to boiling; then reduce heat and simmer, covered, 1½ hours.

Preheat the oven to 350° F. Remove the goose and place on a V-shaped rack in a large roasting pan. Add 4 cups of simmering giblet stock to the roaster, but do not allow the liquid to touch the bottom of goose. Reserve any remaining giblet stock for use in Warm Pears and Chestnuts (recipe follows). Roast the goose in the preheated oven, basting every 15 minutes until brown, about 1 hour. Remove and let stand 10 minutes before carving. Reserve pan juices.

To make the gravy, heat the butter in a large saucepan over medium heat. Whisk in the flour and cook, whisking constantly, until the mixture is light brown in color. Slowly add the reserved pan juices and whisk until smooth. Heat to boiling; reduce heat and simmer, stirring gently, until thick (add more giblet stock if too thick). Stir in the reserved chopped giblets and liver. Keep warm until ready to serve. *Serves 6.*

ABOVE: *We made these silver-pear place cards by writing each guest's name with a glue gun on a fresh pear. The glue must dry completely before the pear can be sprayed.*

WARM PEARS AND CHESTNUTS

1 tablespoon canola oil
1 pound shallots, peeled
1 8-ounce jar roasted chestnuts, halved
1 pound dried pears
1 teaspoon salt
½ teaspoon freshly ground black pepper
1 teaspoon dried marjoram
3 cups reserved giblet stock or chicken broth
2 teaspoons balsamic vinegar

❖ 159 ❖

Heat the oil in a saucepan over medium heat. Add the shallots; cook, turning often, until golden but not brown, about 6 minutes. Add the chestnuts and cook 3 minutes. Add the pears, salt, pepper, and marjoram; toss well. Add the stock and vinegar. Heat to boiling; reduce heat and simmer, covered, about 5 minutes. Remove from heat and keep covered while pears plump and flavors develop.

To serve, spoon around the goose on a serving platter. *Serves 6.*

Grüne Klösse
Potato Dumplings

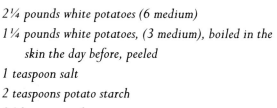

2¼ pounds white potatoes (6 medium)

1¼ pounds white potatoes, (3 medium), boiled in the
    skin the day before, peeled

1 teaspoon salt

2 teaspoons potato starch

24 large toasted croutons

Literally, the German words mean green (raw) dumplings. These potato dumplings are made from a mixture of raw and cooked potatoes and served with gravy. They are also so flavorful and satisfying, it's easy to see why they are traditional in Germany and why each region in Germany claims its own version of this dish to be the best! Germans, in fact, are passionate, almost zealous, about potatoes.

In Vogtland, where Ruth is from, the people are even a bit snobbish about potatoes, claiming to be the first region in all of Germany to receive potatoes from the New World and to begin cultivating them. They grow so well in the region that *Vogtländer* feel that no other region has found as many ways to prepare potato dishes, and that no other region has developed as many uses for potatoes. Each of Ruth's grandmothers came from a different region, and both could make wonderful *Grüne Klösse* in the blink of an eye. But both grandmothers disagreed endlessly about how to do it—one making them with raw potatoes only, the other mixing the raw with boiled. Borrowing from the expertise and passion for potatoes of both grandmothers, here is the official Henderson recipe.

Peel the 2¼ pounds of potatoes and grate into a bowl of salted water to cover.

Fill a large saucepan or stockpot with water and heat to boiling.

Place the grated potatoes in a tightly woven kitchen towel and squeeze out any excess water. Push the cooked potatoes through a ricer and combine with the grated potatoes in a large bowl. Add salt and potato starch and mix well.

Working quickly so that the potatoes don't turn color, pinch off enough potato mixture to shape into a mound about the size of a tennis ball. Using your fingertip, insert 1 or 2 croutons into the center of the ball. Remold to cover the hole. Repeat this process, working quickly and dipping your hands in a bowl of water if they get too sticky. Continue until you've made about 10 dumplings.

Gently drop all the dumplings into the boiling water. When the water returns to a boil, reduce the heat and simmer 15 minutes. The dumplings will eventually float to the top. Remove from heat and let stand another 10 minutes. Transfer with a slotted spoon to a warmed serving bowl. To serve, spoon some dumplings onto each plate and smother with goose gravy. *Makes about 10.*

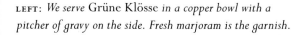

LEFT: *We serve* Grüne Klösse *in a copper bowl with a pitcher of gravy on the side. Fresh marjoram is the garnish.*

RED CABBAGE AND APPLES

This makes enough for the next day's meal as well, so cut the recipe in half if you want less.

¾ pound sliced dried apples

1 quart apple cider or apple juice

4 pounds (about 4 medium heads) red cabbage, cored and finely shredded

Salt and freshly ground pepper to taste

4 tablespoons light brown sugar

¼ cup balsamic vinegar

1 large onion, peeled and stuck with 12 cloves

Place the apples in a medium bowl. Add apple cider, cover, and let stand at least 1 hour or overnight.

Combine the cabbage and apples, with their soaking liquid, and salt and pepper in a large saucepan. Slowly heat to boiling; then reduce heat and simmer. Add the sugar and vinegar and stir well. Place the onion in the center. Cover and simmer 45 minutes. Transfer to a serving bowl, repositioning the onion in the center, or serve right from the saucepan. *Serves 10 to 12.*

ABOVE: *We cook and serve the cabbage in a wonderful old copper pot that had an earlier life at the Algonquin Hotel kitchen in New York City.*

ABOVE: *Dinner is served on preheated plates.*

PISTACHIO ICE CREAM TREE WITH WARM RED CURRANT SAUCE

6 quarts pistachio ice cream, softened
1 quart fresh currants or raspberries
2 cups light brown sugar
6 whole cloves
1 ounce light rum or cognac (optional)
Chocolate sprinkles, nuts, or candy for garnish

Line two 12-cup tree molds with plastic wrap, leaving about 2 inches to overlap the rim. Fill each with ice cream, smoothing the surface with a spatula or knife. Place molds, ice cream surface up, on a baking sheet and freeze 1½ hours. Then place the 2 molds together, pressing the ice cream surfaces together, and secure with rubber bands. Freeze overnight.

Combine the currants, sugar, and cloves in a medium saucepan. Heat to boiling; then reduce heat and cook until reduced by ⅓, about 15 minutes. Skim off the foam as it forms. Add rum or cognac if desired. Keep warm.

To serve, let the tree stand at room temperature 10 minutes. Unmold by dipping the molds into a basin of warm water for a few seconds and pulling gently on the excess plastic. Stand the unmolded tree in a soufflé dish or any other dish deep enough to support the lowest "branches" of the

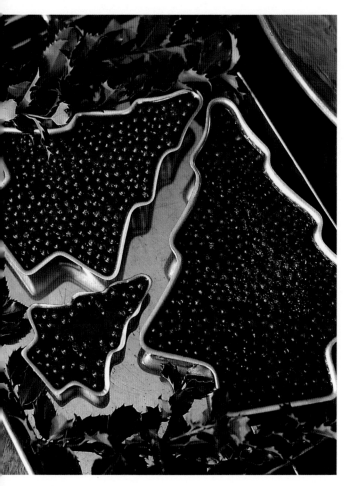

GELATIN DESSERT TREES

We made three of these trees for the kids. They were easy to do and delightful to look at. We used currants, but blueberries work wonderfully also.

2 3-ounce boxes strawberry gelatin mix
Fresh currants or frozen or fresh blueberries (see below for
*   quantity)*

Combine the gelatin mix and 3½ cups boiling water in a large mixing bowl; stir until gelatin is dissolved. Stir in 3½ cups cold water (1 cup less than package directions require). Place the proper amount of berries in each of three tree-shaped molds and fill with the proper amount of warm gelatin mixture (see below). Refrigerate until set, about 5 hours.

To unmold, loosen the edges with a knife and invert the mold onto a serving platter or plate. Lay a steaming hot towel over the mold for 1 minute. Shake gently and remove the mold. *Makes 3 trees— 1 small, 1 medium, and 1 large.*

For small (½-cup) tree mold: 5 tablespoons warm gelatin
*   mixture and 2 tablespoons fresh or frozen blueber-*
*   ries, unthawed*
Medium (1-quart) tree mold: 2 cups warm gelatin mix-
*   ture and 1 cup fresh or frozen blueberries, unthawed*
Large (2-quart) tree mold: 1 quart warm gelatin mixture
*   and 2½ cups fresh or frozen blueberries, unthawed*

৬৯ ২৶

tree. Decorate and garnish with chocolate sprinkles, nuts, or candy. Heat a sharp knife in hot water. Slice off generous portions of ice cream and serve with warm currant sauce. *Serves 10–20.*

৬৯ ২৶

ABOVE LEFT: *To make this tree three-dimensional, we pack ice cream into two molds and put them together. Other possibilities include vanilla ice cream with chocolate sauce or chocolate ice cream with shredded coconut for a "snowy" tree.*

ABOVE: *We serve the gelatin right from the mold because we like how it looks. (Unmold for a more traditional look.) Fresh holly from bushes given to us by the Silo staff over the years provides decoration.*

KAFFEEKLATSCH IN THE AFTERNOON

A Kaffeeklatsch is as much a part of the German social ritual as is afternoon tea to the English. Ruth grew up with this custom of meeting with friends in the late afternoon for steaming coffee, dark cocoa, sweets, and lots of conversation.

Friends and neighbors would always gather with Ruth and her family for the most special Kaffeeklatsch of the year. A holiday stollen, which had been baked weeks before, wrapped tightly, then stored in a wooden box in the cool attic, would make its debut. During those long weeks of Advent, it had developed a special flavor and texture that all at the Kaffeeklatsch would praise while devouring it.

Our modern-day Kaffeeklatsch on the farm keeps this delectable custom alive.

◆165◆

Hunt Hill Stollen

Kartoffelkuchen
POTATO CAKE

FAR LEFT: *Marzipan balls dusted in unsweetened cocoa are served in a compote next to this Meissen coffeepot. The coffee set, in a pattern called Weinlaub, is one of the few things saved from Ruth's household after the war. The hand-embroidered tablecloth belonged to Hildegard Einsiedel, Ruth's mother.*

LEFT: *Extra stollen are ready to be wrapped and sent to various friends.*

HUNT HILL STOLLEN

Unlike the traditional Christmas cake from Ruth's childhood, our stollen is more like a bread than a cake. We don't make it the old-fashioned way, which demands lots of fat and weeks of "curing." We do, though, bake ours a few days before Christmas and keep it cool. We also follow the custom of shaping the loaf to resemble the swaddling clothes wrapped around the Christ Child.

A word to dunkers! Because this stollen is more dry than moist, it's perfect for you.

½ cup dried cherries
1 cup chopped candied lemon peel
1 cup chopped candied orange peel
½ cup plus 2 tablespoons light rum
½ cup warm water
1 cup plus 1 tablespoon sugar
2 packets (¼ ounce each) active dry yeast
2 cups milk
1½ cups (3 sticks) unsalted butter
2 teaspoons salt
Zest of 1 lemon
1 teaspoon almond extract
4 large eggs, lightly beaten
2 cups unbleached flour
1½ cups blanched slivered almonds, chopped
5–7 cups flour
3 tablespoons unsalted butter, melted
½ cup vanilla sugar (available in gourmet shops or see page 41)
Confectioners' sugar for garnish

Combine the cherries and candied fruits in a medium bowl. Add ½ cup rum and toss to coat well. Let stand 1 hour. Drain.

Combine the water and 1 tablespoon sugar in a small bowl. Add the yeast and let stand until bubbly, about 5 minutes.

Scald the milk in a small saucepan over medium-high heat. Pour into a large bowl. Add the butter, 1 cup of the sugar, salt, lemon zest, 2 tablespoons rum, and the almond extract; stir until butter melts and sugar is dissolved. Allow the mixture to cool to lukewarm, about 110° F. Add the yeast mixture and stir. Add the eggs and beat well. Gradually add the flour, almonds, cherries, and candied fruits; beat until smooth. Gradually stir in enough of the flour, 1 cup at a time, to make the dough soft but not sticky.

Turn the dough out onto a floured surface and knead 5 minutes, adding more flour if dough sticks. Shape into a ball and place in a well-buttered bowl. Cover with a clean damp towel and place in a warm, draft-free place until doubled in size, about 2½ hours.

Punch the dough down and place on a floured surface. Cut into three equal portions. Let rest 10 minutes. Flatten each portion with the heel of your hand and shape into an oval of about 8x10 inches. Brush with ⅓ of the melted butter and sprinkle with 1 tablespoon vanilla sugar on each oval. Fold each oval almost in half lengthwise and pinch seams to close. Place seam side down on a baking sheet lined with parchment paper. Cover with a clean, damp towel and let rest in a warm, draft-free place for 1½ hours.

Preheat oven to 350° F. Brush loaves with another ⅓ of the butter and sprinkle with the remaining vanilla sugar. Bake until golden brown, about 45 minutes. Cool on a rack. Brush with the remaining butter and dust with confectioners' sugar. To serve, slice in ½-inch slices and dust once more with confectioners' sugar.

Kartoffelkuchen
Potato Cake

This simple potato cake has a wonderful texture and flavor. It is also light—a perfect bit of sweetness after a big meal.

1 cup sugar

1 cup warm milk

6 packets (¼ ounce each) active dry yeast

1½ pounds potatoes (about 3 large), scrubbed and boiled the day before

4 cups flour

1 cup raisins

1 cup (2 sticks) unsalted butter, melted

2 large eggs, lightly beaten

TOPPING

2 tablespoons cinnamon

6 tablespoons sugar

2 tablespoons unsalted butter, melted

Dissolve a pinch of the sugar in the warm milk in a small bowl. Sprinkle with the yeast; stir and allow to stand 5 minutes.

Peel the potatoes and place in a large bowl. Push through a ricer until smooth. Add the flour, yeast mixture, remaining sugar, raisins, 1 cup melted butter, and eggs. Mix well. Cover with a clean, damp towel and place in a warm, draft-free place for 1 hour until increased in size.

Lightly grease a baking sheet. Punch down the dough and knead lightly 1 minute. Place the dough on the baking sheet and, using your fingers and the heels of your hands, press the dough into the shape of the pan until it comes within 1 inch of all four sides. Cover with a clean, damp towel and keep in a warm, draft-free place for 30 minutes.

Preheat the oven to 400° F.

Combine the cinnamon and the 6 tablespoons

sugar in a small bowl. Brush the dough with 1 tablespoon melted butter and bake 35 minutes. While still warm, brush again with remaining butter and sprinkle evenly with the sugar/cinnamon mixture.

When cool, cut into diamond shapes and arrange in layers on a serving plate.

৯৯ ২

ABOVE: *Remembering Kaffee Trömel, a famous coffeehouse in Ruth's home town, Plauen, we cut the* Kartoffelkuchen *in diamond shapes just as they do there. Kaffee mit Schlag is whipped cream floating on top of coffee—or, if one wishes, on top of a mix of coffee and strong cocoa.*

Ringing and Skiing in the New Year

For many years, we happily spent the days between Christmas and New Year's skiing in Vermont and just having fun. We shared a little house in Waitsfield near Sugarbush Mountain with our good friends Johnny Parente and Skeeter Werner and Jackie and Bob Rose. Practically from the moment we got out of the car from the city, we were on the slopes. Skitch and Johnny were wild ones on the mountain. And when they teamed up with Jack Murphy, who was the manager of the resort, they skied literally all day long, hitting the secret runs and hidden places known only to Jack.

Skitch, along with Peter and Hans Estin, was one of the founders of the Ski Club Ten, an informal private club for a whole group of us. On New Year's Eve, we brought food, balloons, streamers, and music and rang in the New Year all together. Then Armando Orsini, a well-known New York City restaurateur, bought a barn there and turned it into a fabulous restaurant. The food, of course, was hearty Italian and the music of the day was the twist. It became *the* place to celebrate New Year's Eve.

While we celebrated New Year's Eve at Orsini's, a New Year's Day Good Luck Buffet became a tradition at our table. We eventually bought a ski house with Johnny Parente, and the first brunch of the New Year became a meal not to miss at Henderson–Parente lodge. But even then, on New Year's Day, between helpings from the buffet there was still skiing, skiing, skiing.

OPPOSITE, TOP LEFT: *Here we are standing at the top of the lift line in Sugarbush, Vermont.*

OPPOSITE, TOP RIGHT: *Hans is almost ready to try his first skis.*

OPPOSITE, MIDDLE RIGHT: *Nineteen is the winning number for Heidi.*

OPPOSITE, BOTTOM: *Wine and cheese at Castle Rock were brought up the mountain by Armando Orsini. From left to right are Gay Estin, Ann and Armando Orsini, Ruth, Martha Carpenter, and Ann McAlpin.*

❖ 169 ❖

Happy New Year

GREETINGS!

~~~ ~~

Since the years when we spent Christmas week in Sugarbush, Vermont, the days between Christmas and New Year's have usually been spent at the farm, catching our breath and recuperating from a busy Silo and concert season. We settle down to do little things and take the time to read the cards we have received. We read them over and over, especially the ones with pictures of children and animals. Our collection chronicles how our friends and their families have grown over the years. We add this year's to the collection and place them on the piano or the mantel, or clip them on a wire wreath.

In 1990 and '92, however, Skitch and the New York Pops embarked on concert tours of Japan right after Christmas. We took all of our cards along and spent the long flight in good spirits reading them. Because it had been such a busy Advent season, we hadn't sent out our own Christmas cards, so we wrote New Year's cards instead and mailed them from Tokyo. One New Year's Eve we were in Osaka. Skitch led the Japanese audience in a ten-second countdown, Times Square–style, complete with drumroll. The audience participated, clapping wildly and counting out loud. At the stroke of midnight, the orchestra played "Auld Lang Syne" and a very spirited "The Night They Invented Champagne," from *Gigi*.

Since that trip, we have been sending Happy New Year cards instead of Christmas greetings and it's great! It gives us time to read and then respond to the cards we've received. We look forward to reading more cards on the long flights we have planned for future New Year's concerts and sending greetings from wherever we land.

CLOCKWISE FROM TOP: *This is the first card we sent from Hunt Hill Farm, which, in 1968, was still just our weekend home. Below, Hans and Heidi perform in their first puppet show with two of their favorite characters. Below them are greetings from all the Hendersons—Dimitri, Heidi, Skitch with Miss Maude, Ruth, Rebecca, and Hans—in 1980. At the bottom, we are wearing sweaters hand-knitted by the mother of Stein Erickson, our ski pro in Sugarbush, Vermont. To the left are Isaac and Vera Stern with their children, David, Michael, and Shira, wishing us a peaceful 1974 from the stage of Carnegie Hall. Above, in 1984, we sent a collage of the year's happy events—here we are with Hans in St. Moritz, where we had a reunion with Ruth's kindergarten class from Plauen, and hugging Heidi after our first New Yorks Pops Gala in spring 1983.*

ALL-WE-GOT-FOR-CHRISTMAS
NEW YEAR'S DAY BUFFET

We consider it the best of luck to get together with friends on New Year's Day wherever we are. Last year we were able to gather in the Silo Cooking School, since New Year's is one of the four days it's closed. We had a great time making use of the big kitchen, cooking on all burners! We offered a buffet put together from gifts of Christmas food we had received from friends all over the country—grapefruit from Florida, ham from our friends the Doughertys at the Egg and I Farm, those wonderfully huge Wolferman's muffins from Kansas City, and a gift basket of homemade cookies. We filled out the menu with potatoes, deviled eggs, and marzipan pigs for good luck.

Florida Grapefruit with Cranberry-Ginger Topping

Spicy Glazed Ham

Himmel und Erde
HEAVEN AND EARTH

Apple Butter Cheddar Muffins

Lady Apple Butter

Candy-Cane Cookies

Lemon Snowballs

Chocolate Hearts

◆ 173 ◆

FAR LEFT: *A hand-carved pig is featured on the buffet. A shadow-box creation by Erik Erikson and a wreath of dried peppers warm the walls. Himmel und Erde, baked ham garnished with mini-oranges, lady apples, and rosemary, and deviled eggs, cut so they sit upright, all taste good at room temperature.* LEFT: *The New Year's buffet is self-contained on our big tavern table. The clock is one of Skitch's favorites—he had it electrified for the cooking school, knowing how we might forget to wind it.*

Florida Grapefruit with Cranberry-Ginger Topping

4 cups fresh cranberries, washed and picked over
¼ cup water
1 cup honey
¼ cup minced crystallized ginger
2 cinnamon sticks
4 medium grapefruit

Combine the cranberries and water in a saucepan. Heat to boiling over medium heat. Add the honey, ginger, and cinnamon sticks. Return mixture to boiling while stirring constantly. Reduce heat and simmer 15 minutes.

Cut the grapefruit in half. Using a small serrated knife, remove the sections, pith, and seeds. Return the sections to the grapefruit halves. Top with cranberry mixture. *Serves 8*.

ৎৡ ৵

Spicy Glazed Ham

1 15-pound precooked ham
½ cup apple cider
8 ounces prepared honey mustard
10 ounces pepper jelly
Juice of 1 lemon
5 teaspoons cream-style prepared horseradish

Preheat oven to 350° F.

Place the ham on a rack in a roasting pan. Add cider to the bottom of pan.

Combine the honey mustard, pepper jelly, lemon juice, and horseradish in a small bowl. Spread half of this mixture over ham and cover loosely with aluminum foil. Place the ham in the oven until warmed through, about 1 hour.

To serve, cut into slices and pass extra honey mustard glaze on the side. *Serves 8*.

ৎৡ ৵

ABOVE: *We slice some of the ham so it's ready to serve and leave the carving set for those who want seconds.*

Himmel und Erde
Heaven and Earth

This is a simple and eloquent marriage of potato and apple. Truly German!

1 tablespoon cider vinegar
8 medium potatoes, peeled and quartered
8 apples, cored, peeled, and quartered
½ pound bacon, diced
4 medium onions, peeled and thinly sliced
Sprigs of fresh parsley for garnish

Fill a large stockpot with boiling water. Add vinegar, then the potatoes and apples. Cook until soft, about 15 to 20 minutes. Drain.

Meanwhile, cook the bacon in a large heavy skillet until brown and crisp; remove and drain on paper towel. Add the onions to the same skillet; cook until crisp and very dark in color (almost black). Cool. Combine the onions and bacon in a small bowl.

Place the potatoes and apples in a serving bowl. Sprinkle bacon and onions over the top. Garnish with parsley. *Serves 8–10.*

৯৯ ২৬

APPLE BUTTER CHEDDAR MUFFINS

Wolferman's in Kansas City does a fabulous mail-order business at Christmastime. We love this present—a box of their huge muffins! This year it was a sampler—loaded with six different varieties. Of course, this recipe will work with other brands of English muffin—try it with whole-wheat muffins too.

8 Wolferman's English muffins
Lady Apple Butter (recipe follows)
8 ounces Vermont cheddar cheese, grated

Preheat broiler.

Gently separate the muffins into halves using a fork or English-muffin cutter. Spread each half evenly with apple butter and place on a baking sheet. Sprinkle tops with cheese. Place under broiler until cheese is melted and bubbly. *Serves 8.*

৯৯ ২৬

LADY APPLE BUTTER

Made from our own local harvest of tiny lady apples, this spread is also great when made from other varieties of tart apples.

½ peck lady apples, washed
1 cup water
1 cup apple cider
Juice of 2 lemons
2 teaspoons cinnamon
1 teaspoon allspice
1 cup sorghum molasses or blackstrap molasses

If using apples other than lady apples, cut into quarters, but do not core or seed. Cook the whole lady apples or the quartered larger apples in the water in a large saucepan over medium heat until soft, about 30 minutes. Push apples through a food mill and place pulp in a saucepan. Add the cider, lemon juice, cinnamon, allspice, and molasses. Slowly heat to boiling, stirring constantly. Reduce heat and simmer until apple butter reaches desired consistency (we like ours so you can spoon it), about 20 minutes. Simmer longer if you like it thicker. Pour into hot sterilized pint jars, leaving ¼-inch space at the top. Seal and place in a large pot filled with gently boiling hot water. The water must cover the jars by 1 inch. Simmer gently at least 10 minutes. Cool and store in a cool dry place. *Makes 3 pints.*

৯৯ ২৬

CANDY-CANE COOKIES

2 cups flour
½ teaspoon salt
¼ teaspoon baking powder
¾ cup (1½ sticks) unsalted butter, softened
¾ cup sugar
1 large egg, lightly beaten
½ teaspoon vanilla extract
½ teaspoon peppermint extract
⅓ cup flaked coconut
1 teaspoon red food coloring

Sift the flour, salt, and baking powder together in a bowl. Set aside.

Beat the butter and sugar in the bowl of an electric mixer until light. Add the egg, vanilla, and peppermint extract, beating well after each addition. Gradually add flour mixture, beating until a soft dough forms.

Divide the dough in half and place each portion in a separate bowl. Stir the coconut into one half and the food coloring into the other. Cover with plastic wrap and chill 1 hour.

Preheat the oven to 375° F. Lightly grease a cookie sheet.

Divide the coconut dough into 15 equal portions and shape into balls. Do the same with the red dough. Using your hands, gently roll a white ball on a lightly floured board into a thin rope 6 inches long. Do the same with a red ball. Pinch one end of the white rope and one end of the red rope together.

Carefully twist white and red ropes around each other to create candy-cane stripes. Pinch closed at the other end. Place on the prepared cookie sheet and bend the top portion over to form the crook of a cane. Repeat this process until the cookie sheet is filled with candy canes placed

◆176◆

about ¾ inch apart. Bake until white part is barely golden, about 10 minutes.

Cool on a rack. *Makes 15.*

˜˜˜

ABOVE: *In addition to the cookies we've included recipes for here, Sandy's cookie gift basket included her favorite ginger animals, sugar stars, trees, and ginger people. She used cellophane to wrap the cookies first, then added some fresh evergreens, then wrapped the whole basket with more cellophane.*

LEMON SNOWBALLS

1¾ cups flour
¼ teaspoon baking powder
¼ teaspoon cream of tartar
½ teaspoon salt
½ cup (1 stick) unsalted butter, softened
⅔ cup sugar
2 teaspoons grated lemon rind
1 large egg
Juice of 1½ lemons (about 3 tablespoons) or 1 teaspoon
    lemon extract
1 tablespoon water
½ cup finely chopped walnuts
½ cup confectioners' sugar, or more if necessary

Sift the flour, baking powder, cream of tartar, and salt together in a bowl. Set aside.

Beat the butter and sugar in the bowl of an electric mixer until light. Add the lemon rind, egg, lemon juice, and water, beating well after each addition. Gradually add the flour mixture, beating until a soft dough forms. Stir in the nuts. Cover with plastic wrap and chill 1 hour.

Preheat the oven to 350° F.

Form the dough into 1-inch balls and place 1 inch apart on an ungreased cookie sheet. Bake until lightly golden, about 10 minutes.

Place the confectioners' sugar in a small bowl.

While they are still warm, roll cookies in the sugar to cover. Add more sugar when needed. Cool on a rack. *Makes 2 dozen.*

ॐ ॐ

CHOCOLATE HEARTS

1½ cups flour
⅔ cup McStevie's Spicy Cocoa or sweetened cocoa powder
½ teaspoon baking powder
½ teaspoon baking soda
¼ teaspoon salt
½ cup (1 stick) unsalted butter, softened
¾ cup sugar
1 large egg, lightly beaten
1 teaspoon vanilla extract
Multicolored sugar crystals for garnish

Sift the flour, cocoa, baking powder, soda, and salt together in a bowl. Set aside.

Beat the butter and sugar in the bowl of an electric mixer until light. Add the egg and vanilla, beating well after each addition. Gradually add the flour mixture, beating until a soft dough forms. Divide the dough into 3 equal portions and shape each into a brick. Cover with plastic wrap and chill overnight.

Preheat the oven to 325° F. Lightly grease a cookie sheet.

Roll out one portion of dough on a lightly floured surface to ⅛-inch thickness. Using a 3-inch heart-shaped cookie cutter (or two different-size heart-shaped cutters), cut cookies from dough and place on prepared cookie sheet about ½ inch apart. Sprinkle with sugar crystals. Repeat process with the other portions of dough. Bake 5 to 7 minutes. Allow to cool slightly before removing from the cookie sheet. Cool completely on a wire rack. *Makes 3 dozen.*

ॐ ॐ

. . . AND A PIG FOR LUCK

For Germans, the symbols for good luck for the New Year are pigs and four-leaf clovers. To give one or both to someone on New Year's Day is to wish that person the best of everything in the coming year. The gift of a marzipan pig with a four-leaf clover in its mouth or in a slit on its back, like the one on top of a savings bank, will surely multiply your fortunes.

Our New Year's Buffet table is wild with pigs—a large wooden carved pig, a painted pig, pig napkin rings, and, of course, dozens of small marzipan pigs we found in a shop in the Yorkville section of New York City. But there's nothing like taking a good walk up the road to Nancy and Jim Dougherty's pig farm, where we can rub a real pig for good luck. Visiting the pigs is a wonderful experience. Whenever you think you have seen the biggest one ever, you turn and look and there is an even bigger one. Absolutely irresistible are the piglets. Jim holds one up for us. We delight in giving the piglet a little rub while wishing out loud—to our neighbors, family, and friends—health, wealth, and good fortune! Forever!

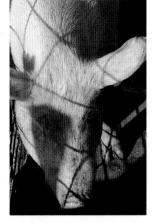

FAR LEFT: *One of Jim Dougherty's pigs at the Egg and I Farm has plunked herself on the threshold of the pen, blocking the exit for others.*

ABOVE: *Some of Jim's pigs enjoy the winter sun.*

Index

Italicized page number indicates illustration.

The New York Pops Christmas in the Country
A NOTE FROM SKITCH HENDERSON, FOUNDER & MUSIC DIRECTOR

There is a cavernous ballroom on the West Side of New York called Manhattan Center, which was *the* place to be seen, even before Roseland. By itself, it can give a history lesson not only in the theater of the 1930s and 40s but in the songs of the big bands, which we danced to during World War II. Next door, the Hotel New Yorker showcased Artie Shaw and his orchestra.

Into this realm of memories, The New York Pops gathered in April 1993 to recreate the Christmas holiday with 80 players—give or take a few, depending upon repertoire. Can you imagine singing "Jingle Bells" on a warm spring day? Jimmy Van Heusen of Hollywood film fame was once told to write a melody for a song called "Christmas in July." We were roommates at the time and I vividly recall our discussion of music for the holidays and its fads and foibles.

After adjusting all the technical equipment to the engineer's comfort (this took 35 minutes), we began to record. Then a strange thing took place: it became Christmas!

Recording is a slow and laborious job. A chair squeaked. The old ballroom floor groaned at the wrong moment. Ancient water pipes chimed in with their songs. But in spite of it all, we made Christmas come alive.

Our holiday concerts at Carnegie Hall have taught me that traditional music for the holidays is your preference. In this recording, we bring you a variety of traditional songs, diverse both in orchestral color and in musical style.

Our Christmas began in April, but now it's here for you to enjoy. We can't be there to hang your stocking, but this recording should put you in the mood.

ABOUT THE NEW YORK POPS

The New York Pops was founded in 1983 by Skitch Henderson to give New York a permanent, professional pops orchestra specializing in American popular and symphonic repertoire. Its mission is to broaden public appreciation and enjoyment of America's rich musical heritage.

The center of The New York Pops' activity is a concert series at Carnegie Hall. The orchestra also moves easily from the concert hall to the heart of the city, where thousands of New Yorkers enjoy free outdoor performances. In addition, The New York Pops tours nationally and internationally.

The New York Pops' unique education programs encourage the musical aspirations of young people and offer an opportunity to experience symphonic pops music firsthand. The orchestra, which is composed of some of New York's finest musicians, is the largest independent pops orchestra in the United States today.

The Angel recording series includes *From Berlin to Bernstein* and *The New York Pops Goes to the Movies*.

• •

Joy to the World	4:17	*Christmas Fantasy*	3:02
Georg Friedrich Handel		*Hark the Herald Angels Sing*	
Arranger: Carmen Dragon, Dragon Music Co.		**Felix Mendelssohn - Bartholdy**	
Toyland / March of the Toys	4:52	*Silent Night*	
Victor Herbert		**Franz Gruber**	
Arranger: Ralph Hermann		*Jingle Bells*	
Carol of the Drum	3:09	**James Pierpont**	
Katherine K. Davis		Arrangers: Skitch Henderson & Ralph Hermann	
Publisher: Milis Music Inc.; Arranger: Ray Wright		*Carol of the Bells*	2:42
Oh, Tannenbaum	3:13	**M. Leontovich**	
Traditional German		Arranger: Richard Hayman	
Arranger: Skitch Henderson		*Merry Christmas*	2:38
Parade of the Wooden Soldiers	3:48	**Traditional 16th Century**	
Leon Jessel		Arranger: Skitch Henderson	
Arranger: Ralph Hermann		*Deck the Halls*	3:11
Der Schneemann	4:39	**Traditional Welsh**	
Erich Korngold		Arranger: Carmen Dragon, Dragon Music Co.	
Dream Pantomime fr. Hänsel & Gretel	4:52		
Engelbert Humperdinck			

Producer: Thomas Frost • Engineer: Thomas Lazarus • Recorded at Manhattan Center Studios on April 5 & 6, 1993

The New York Pops wishes to thank Leon H. Charney
for his generous support of the orchestra's efforts.

SPECIAL VALUE

Original Price
SPECIAL $14.98
084006513-2

N 0795 B&N RUTH SKITCH HENDER

75% OFF